Contents

Knowledge As Desire

AN ESSAY ON FREUD AND PIAGET

Hans G. Furth

COLUMBIA UNIVERSITY PRESS

New York

Library of Congress Cataloging-in-Publication Data

Furth, Hans G.
  Knowledge as desire.

Bibliography: p.
  Includes index.
  1. Symbolism (psychology) in children.   2. Desire.
3. Knowledge, Theory of.   4. Logic.   5. Freud, Sigmund,
1856–1939.   6. Piaget, Jean, 1896–1980.   I. Title.
BF723.S94F87   1987   153.5   86-23278
ISBN 0-231-06458-6
ISBN 0-231-06459-4 (pbk.)

Columbia University Press
New York   Oxford

Printed in the United States of America

c 10 9 8 7 6 5 4 3 2 1
p 10 9 8 7 6 5 4 3 2 1

Preface to
the Paperback Edition

THE 1990 PUBLICATION of a paperback edition provides the welcome opportunity to share with the readers some further implications of this essay's integration of Freud and Piaget. In order to ground a radically constructivist viewpoint that links society and the individual, two related issues need to be expanded and redirected into societal directions. Having proposed a libidinal "want-my-object" underlying all mental life from its beginning, it remains to explain how the pleasure of satisfying a want relates to the construction of societal relations. Second, it is insufficient to describe the object in terms of face-to-face interpersonal experiences: child-parent or friendship relations by themselves lack the requisite quality to transform into societal relations. In other words, I propose now that the "object" of Piaget's object formation in its most general meaning is precisely "a societal world," such that, regardless of specific and concrete societal influences impinging on the developing child, there is the spontaneous tendency within children to construct societal relations. Likewise, their "want" is not so much the seeking of pleasure for its own sake as the desire to ground their mental life in a societal form.

In a recent interchange of ideas I spelled out these notions in greater detail.[1] As there was a need for a synthesis making it possible, indeed obligatory, to recognize logic in libido and, vice versa, libido in logic, so it seemed to me we need a dialectical viewpoint that links society and the person.

For this purpose it is not much of an explanation to describe the person-society relation as an innate human tendency toward sociality when it is just as legitimate and obligatory to state the reverse, that each person is already a societal institution. In positing the radical imaginary as the source of society Castoriadis has advanced a clarifying viewpoint, albeit by appealing to a psychological capacity that itself is not generally recognized or well defined.[2] When I continue Castoriadis' efforts and equate the radical imaginary with the psychological constructs of objects and images, I cannot flatter myself to refer to capacities recognized by all psychologists. Nevertheless I adapted Piaget's and Freud's theories to make these capabilities comprehensible: Piaget's theory, with respect to the logical status of the mental object and the symbolic image; Freud's theory with respect to the libidinal dynamics motivating their construction. In my view, a libidinal "want-my-object" is at the base of all object thinking.

In this connection I was puzzled that evolution would have selected the pleasure principle almost as an end in itself. I speculated then that the function of the pleasure principle is in fact the construction of an interpersonal symbolic life, characteristic of all humans, and that in adults it is present in a pre-socialized unconscious and in a partially socialized conscious. In this manner it can be said the pleasure principle is at the base of interpersonal relations and personhood. But I had misgivings about these speculations, precisely because they left society outside interpersonal relations and would lead to the possibility of postulating the person prior to society.

At this point in my thinking I encountered Castoriadis' thesis on the imaginary institution of society. Trying to understand the meaning of the radical imaginary, I concluded that it was indeed identical with the capability to create objects and symbols, the place where, as I put it, Freud and Piaget, libido and logic meet. But now I realized that the object of "want-my-object" is not simply the pleasure of personal feelings or interpersonal relations. No, the object that the child desires and imagines is from the time of the very first construction (that is, in my framework, around age two) precisely the human society. Quite literally, children's favorite occupation is what Castoriadis calls the imaginary institution of society. They do this spontaneously in their thinking, imagining, and symbolic play. They are driven to do it and they do it "for fun." Most important for consensual evaluation, this activity can at least be partially observed in children's spontaneous play and verbalizations.

Observe any two children, age four to six, engaged in pretend play and one does not fail to notice societal roles, norms, values, and ideologies. The content is of course taken from the particular culture in which the children live and no doubt at times specific children may reenact some personal emotionally-laden event of their own history. But throughout the most varied situations the imitated contents are assimilated to the general form of what I call imaginary micro-societies, playful to us observers, deadly serious to the children, as if their life depended on it—as indeed it does. For without society there is no person.

If it seems reasonable to regard children's pretend play and fantasy as a first attempt to construct and be libidinally attached to societal institutions, then indeed this activity can be seen to have a most basic evolutionary function, namely, to create the psychological framework, both cognitive and emotional, to make human societies possible. This is something different from the common opinion that children's play is "in the main a rehearsal for the skills necessary to function within a given culture." For example, it is hard to imagine in what sense playing airplane prepares a boy for the technical or social skills of flying. My claim is also quite different from the postulation of innate ideas; on the contrary, these "childish" ideas have to be

constructed by children themselves in the course of their individual development. The content, as said before, is of course
taken from the available culture, but the selection and the
meaning and the value given to these cultural elements are the
children's own doing. And what is the name of this psychological ability to give new meaning and value? It is precisely the
capability to create objects and symbols, which children develop
around age two.

From this perspective, the peculiarity of the human
libido and its pervasive pleasure principle make evolutionary
sense. For now the biological function of this innate drive to
create objects of desire can be spelled out: It is the instituting of
a societal world. In other words, human evolution can be said
to have selected the capacity to create objects and symbols so
as to prepare humans developmentally for societal institutions,
at the same time as it prepares them for personhood.

ENDNOTES

1. Furth, G. H. 1989. Reply. *Human Development,* 32:6. What follows in
the text is taken from this rejoinder.
2. Castoriadis, C. 1987. *The Imaginary Institution of Society.* Cambridge:
MIT Press.

TO THE READER

THIS ESSAY HAS a few quite specific aims even though it covers a great variety of matters that can be treated in much greater detail within specific academic sub-disciplines. In order to help you not to lose sight of the overall direction it may be helpful to state the major objectives in the following points:

1. First, I elucidate Piaget's theory of object knowledge, specifically the developmental origin of theoretical knowledge in the transition from the object-of-action to the object-of-knowledge. As a consequence of object knowledge symbolic representation becomes psychologically available and developmentally comprehensible.

2. Second, I accept the main themes of Freud's theory as part of normal psychology and interpret them within Piaget's developmental framework. At the same time I point out that behind any symbol- and knowledge-formation (even the most "objective") there is ultimately an obligatory personal motivation of "I-want-my-object."

3. As a result of this synthesis Piaget's theory of knowledge is shown to be radically social and emotional, contrary

to what is commonly assumed; while conversely Freud's observations on repression, the id, the unconscious, eros and death drive become demystified in the clearly articulated history of individual knowledge development.

4. Fourth, I meet some tough epistemological questions head on and speculate on some possible solutions. With Freud I focus on childhood sexuality as uniquely characteristic of evolving humanity; with Piaget I attempt to overcome the apparent contradiction between a contingent evolutionary history and a logically necessary objective knowledge.

In the final analysis this entire essay is a sketch to overcome the baneful split between knowledge and emotion, between mental operation and interpersonal cooperation, by presenting the inextricable interaction of logic (knowledge) and sexuality (desire) from the very first developmental beginnings in human symbol formation.

1.

Symbols: Where Freud and Piaget Meet

"DESIRE EXISTS ONLY when the object exists; the object exists only when desire exists; desire and object are a pair of twins, neither of which can come into the world the least moment before the other."

This cry of Kierkegaard, taken up by modern existential philosophy, strikes a deep chord in the heart of many contemporaries. Yet to these same people, objects of knowledge and of desire are anything but two sides of the same coin. Emotion and intellect are generally seen as separate psychological compartments, both in our personal lives and in our social institutions. In fact, they are frequently considered as antagonistic forces, working against each other. "Alienation" is a favorite description of the existential situation of modern people. Whatever contributes to the composite picture of this state of not being at-one, surely one of its more basic ingredients is that split between desire and knowledge.

What then shall we make of Kierkegaard's comment? What is the source of its attraction? Is it but an idle dream of an unattainable psychological unity, itself generated by unappeased emotions? Or is this wholeness an ideal, a rare phenomenon, occassionally found in some saints or artists, the prerogative of a selected few, but certainly not the birthright of ordinary humans?

Freud, who had very much respect for art and very little for organized religion, did not hesitate to refer to this experience of unity and harmony as an illusion, a constructive and therapeutic illusion in the case of art, an illusion of emotional immaturity in the case of religion. In both instances, Freud thought, psychological factors are at work, deeply buried in the unconscious psychology of the individuals involved, forces that are connected to their earliest emotional life. In stark contrast to the unconscious and its emotional derivatives, he placed the conscious intellect and what he considered its most conspicuous achievement: modern Western science. Scientific thinking and emotional life were clearly separated.

Moreover, Freud envisaged no easy *modus vivendi* between the intellect and the emotions. He referred to a lifelong struggle between the *ego* and the *id*, or as he expressed himself later on between the eros drive and the death drive. Nevertheless, he did permit himself the expression of a guarded optimism and thought that in the long run the constructive intellect would succeed in taming the unruly chaos of the unconscious id: "The primacy of the intellect certainly lies in a far, far distant, but probably not infinite future" (1927 14:377). Apparently, Freud's theoretical perspective remains enclosed in a dualism where the unconscious desires of the emotions and the conscious knowledge of the intellect are in existential conflict. Even his hoped-for solution to this conflict does not change the adversarial relationship of the ego and the id; through the intellect's domination a precarious coexistence, not a constructive unity, is achieved.

Only one other psychologist has attained a worldwide stature anywhere near Freud's. While Freud's psychology is almost exclusively centered on emotions, Piaget's is centered on the intellect. But how are we to explain Piaget's popularity? The nature of the intellect is hardly a burning concern of educated people in general. In fact, Piaget's theory is attractive to many because it is correctly seen as a theory primarily of development, in the same biological sense in which Darwin's theory is an account of the historical evolution of species. Development, however, is very much a modern notion appealing to our sense of emancipation and the autonomous self. What develops, Piaget claimed, happens to be the intellect, or more precisely, as we shall see in great detail later on, the general logical structures of the intellect.

Freud's theories speak to the interest of those trying to understand the less conscious and less controlled components of human actions, and the linkage of development and emotions is a key component of this understanding. In a similiar way, I think, Piaget's theory appeals to many on account of his linking development and knowledge. What is lacking, however, for a fruitful understanding of either theory is a whole picture that directly links knowledge and emotions. The split between these two is an unwholesome state of affairs, whether in personal experience or in articulated or scientific description. This is all the more unsatisfactory in view of the potential unity and constructive role of the science of psychology. It appears, at least to me, something of a scandal that the two most widely known psychologists, Freud and Piaget, have only the most superficial point of contact. Do they, in fact, refer to the same human being? In any case, both are currently interpreted as sanctioning this baneful compartmentalization of knowledge and desire.

Yet is this a just appreciation of Piaget's position? Is there really no organic connection between his theory of knowledge and the psychological reality of emotions? When Piaget was seventy-three years old, he was interviewed for a French television series (Bringuier 1980). He was asked how one can be interested in children and the development of their intelligence alone and not be interested in the affective side? Can they be separated? Piaget's reply was:

"Obviously for intelligence to function, it must be motivated by an affective power. A person won't ever solve a problem if the problem doesn't interest him. The impetus for everything lies in interest, affective motivation. . . . But take, for instance, two boys and their arithmetic lessons. One boy likes them and forges ahead; the other . . . feels inferior and has all the typical complexes of people who are weak in math. The first boy will learn more quickly, the second more slowly. But for both, two and two are four. Affectivity doesn't modify the acquired structure at all. If the problem at hand is the construction of structures, affectivity is essential as a motivation, of course, but it doesn't explain the structures."

The interviewer expressed his astonishment "that affectivity doesn't appear at the level of structures, regardless! An individual is a whole." To which Piaget replied:

"Yes, but in the study of feelings, when you find structures, they are structures of knowledge. For example, in feelings of mutual affection there's an element of comprehension and an element of perception. That's all cognitive. In behavior you have— and I think all scholars are agreed on this point—a structure of behavior and a motivating force of behavior. There is motivation on the one hand, and mechanisms [of structures] on the other."

"And you are interested in mechanism?"

"That's right, yes."

"But if everyone conforms to structures, as you say, don't you lose sight of individuality, of the unique qualities of each person?"

"You're forgetting what I told you about accommodation. There is a great diversity in structures. And the same structures found in different individuals."

"Everyone has his own style of accommodation?"

"Of course. Accommodation gives rise to unlimited differentiations. The same structures are very general. The fact that a number is the same for everyone, and the series of whole numbers is the same for everyone, doesn't prevent mathematicians, taken one by one, from being unique as individuals. There is such diversification of structures . . ."

At this point the interviewer stopped short, wondering whether it is meaningful to reduce the individual to "accommodation." Similar misgivings have been expressed by various authors on different occasions, and these in part explain why Piaget's theory is liable to be misunderstood and misapplied ("It's pretty catastrophic when I see how I'm understood" said Piaget shortly after the above remarks). But the real loss, I feel, has very little to do with one particular theory or the acceptance or rejection of one creative scholar. What really counts here is society's general notion of what persons are and of their psychological capabilities. This certainly is, or should be, a chief concern of the psychological and social sciences, but not theirs alone. These ideas are not limited to the affairs of scholars. All people carry within them implicit notions of persons, of knowledge, emotion and human development. In whatever indirect ways, these notions are part of our daily lives and affect our multiple interpersonal relations from the smallest to the largest extension in space and time.

We heard Piaget's remarks: "In the study of feelings, when you find structures, they are structures of knowledge" and, "The same structures give rise to unlimited differentiation . . . different individuals with their own style of accommodation." It seems challenging to explore Piaget's theory of development with a view toward what he called the motivational base of individual accommodations behind all forms of knowledge. And where could one find a more elementary motivational force than in what Freud called *libido* or the *eros* drive? *Libido* is the Latin word for "desire," more particularly sexual desire. Its general meaning is plain. The same cannot be said for the other of Kierkegaard's pair of twins: namely, "the object." A preliminary elucidation of this term is in order which will set the stage for this entire essay.

OBJECT KNOWLEDGE

For this purpose I invite the reader to reflect on a general cognitive ability fundamental and pervasive in all adult psychology. It is as much part of our mental actions as gravity or the air that surrounds our physical actions. I am referring here to the ability to form what philosophers of old used to call *objects* and to the momentous psychological consequences for human psychology. Since *object* has today quite a different connotation, your reaction to this statement may well be similar to the European peasants, who were intrigued to learn that all along they had been speaking prose. To our way of thinking, we do not form objects; rather we perceive or observe them and in language we name them and can treat them as concepts. As for the existence of objects, we tend to take them for granted, as things or facts out there, certainly not as something that we form.

Why then do I resurrect the old philosophical connotation of the word object and even introduce it as the key perspective in approaching the psychologies of Freud and Piaget? It is known that the meaning of *object* has in fact undergone a radical change in the course of the nineteenth century, so much so that there is really no readily available word in the English language for expressing its original meaning. The other reason is that both Freud and Piaget—still heirs to the continental tradition—did not hesitate to use the object concept in a sense that is much closer to the philosophical past than to the present English usage. While they certainly differed from each other in their respective emphases—the one stressing the emotional-libidinal attachment between two separate persons, the other the cognitive construction of a person vis-à-vis a separate object-of-knowledge—these differences dwindle compared to the much more basic similarity in their understanding of the word *object*. In this matter both Freud and Piaget talked of the formation of objects; both insisted that persons are actively doing something in establishing objects and that this doing has a personal and developmental history. It would be fair to say that for both scholars objects—whether objects of attachment or objects of knowledge—imply personal relations on the part of agents who construct these objects.

This capability to form objects, singled out in the preceeding paragraphs, is critically related to Piaget's and Freud's use of that word. Objects as products of personal construction is a fundamentally different notion than objects as things. Part of the difficulty of understanding their theoretical positions is probably due to the above mentioned change in meaning, which in its most extreme form contrasts objects-as-known, that is, object *knowledge*, with objects-as-things, that is, *facts*.

However, my aim here is not to engage in philosophical disputes about knowledge and knowledge claims, even though there is no good way to avoid getting involved to a certain extent. But this is left to later chapters. Rather, the purpose of these introductory remarks is to suggest a perspective that firmly links knowledge and action, as Piaget does with regard to the sensorimotor stage of development. At that stage knowledge is not something apart from action; it is conceptualized as an implicit component within the action. So there is action knowledge but not yet object knowledge. Piaget then studied in meticulous detail how infants during the first two years of their life acquire object knowledge. In this manner he turned philosophical speculation about knowledge into an empirical study. The concept of *object* became anchored in a psychological description of its observable acquisition and its subsequent expansion within an overall theory of knowledge development.

Piaget's originality, I believe, consists to a large part in showing a developmental continuity between the sensorimotor knowledge of infants and the objective knowledge of adults and scientists. In this developmental passage, starting around age two, object knowledge and its psychological repercussions play a crucial role. As a direct consequence of Piaget's empirical procedure—of observing in a controlled and systematic fashion the beginnings of what would eventually become adult "objective" knowledge—his theory of knowledge is bound to the biological and human context in a different way than abstract philosophical theories.

What then is this object knowledge, which Piaget claims has its beginning around age two? He defined it as action-differentiated knowledge, a definition not easily comprehended, which the next chapter will attempt to remedy. Suffice it to say that *object knowledge* refers to a type of knowledge through which we can make absent events mentally present to ourselves. The important thing at the moment is to grasp that the ability to form objects is a developmental acquisition that cannot be taken for granted.

However, since this concept of object is unfamiliar to

today's readers, is there no other word meaningful in everyday language, a word that could carry us along to the point where the philosophical connotation of object can be incorporated into an empirical theory of knowledge development? I implied earlier that object formation brought about crucial changes in the child's psychology. Would it not be possible to describe these changes with a common word and then use this word as a suitable substitute to indicate the ability to form objects? This is precisely what I plan to do except that now I find a great variety of possible choices, whereas in the case of the philosophical concept of *object* I was at a loss for even a single other word.

DIFFERENT FORMS OF SYMBOLS

For reasons that will be spelled out in detail in the next chapter, I suggest here the use of the words *symbol, symbolic* and *to symbolize* to indicate what is implied by object knowledge and its consequences. Unfortunately, the word *symbol* means different things to different people; but this is the case with every other possible vocabulary. Right now it is important for the reader not to limit the meaning of *symbol* only to something that has an obscure or hidden meaning (this is how Freud used the word). But provisionally let it stand for any psychological situation that has meaning beyond its immediate action presence. Your sitting on the chair at present is in itself not a symbolic, but a present nonsymbolic action; however, speaking about it, a mental image, a gesture, a drawing, a fantasy, or a dream about it would all be included as different forms of symbols.

In this example various situations were listed, all of which have in common their being different forms of symbolic acts. All are related to this fundamental object capability for which we are attempting to find a comprehensible English vocabulary. The words *image, imagery, imagination,* and *imaging* come to mind. The drawback is that they are connected with the visual image, which in turn implies the perception of something seen. There is an almost irresistible tendency to think of knowledge in terms of a picture, an internal copy of what is out there. This tendency has to be vigorously resisted, and no better remedy against it can be provided than the case of children totally blind from birth, yet perfectly able to perceive and imagine—yet obviously not in the visual modality.

Another word is *representation,* especially when it is hyphenated to stress the aspect of reconstruction: *to re-present,* i.e., to make present again, in the absence of the original event. On the negative side, it is, like object, a technical term invented by philosophers and is often used in a specific sense to distinguish kinds of symbols, such as *representative,* meaning "conventional" as opposed to *non-representative,* meaning "idiosyncratic" symbols. On the other hand, it is now also quite common to take representation in a very broad sense so that it becomes strictly synonymous with all forms of internal knowledge(—which actually means all forms of knowledge since a knowledge that would *not* be internal does not make sense).

Some other words are conceivable as possible vocabulary to stand for object knowledge, such as *fantasy* and *language.* *Fantasy* is not a bad word for present purposes, especially since in a developmental perspective children's object knowledge very quickly and most conspicuously shows itself in symbolic play and internal fantasy. But in a more global sense, the word is too much connected with internal, nonobjective and noncontrolled features to be a suitable description for a variety of symbolic acts, including those that are external and also logically and socially controlled. The word *language* in the form of *inner language,* likewise, would be a suitable candidate. It has a social connotation that is good and also a desirable interpersonal component. But this use could lead to a serious conceptual confusion between knowledge and language; moreover, the phenomenon of societal language should be studied in its own right without linking it to specific knowledge functions.

Symbolic knowledge appears therefore to be the most comprehensible as well as comprehensive description for the general psychological ability that is inherently connected to what Piaget's theory calls object knowledge. This symbolic ability is responsible for the fact that all persons, wherever else they may live, live in a symbolic world. Symbols are in fact the most direct result of object knowledge, and a good part of this essay will deal with the symbolic life as it develops in children. If this is the case, why, you may ask, did I not omit the difficult concept of *object* and straight away focus on symbols? Because one major aim of this essay is precisely to elucidate how the ability to form symbols comes about. In the attempt at explaining the genesis of symbols, I will make use of the theories of Piaget and of Freud. As a first step I will attempt to substantiate the claim that Piaget's theory provides an empirical explanation for how children develop this symbolic power during their first years. This explanation, however, rests on an understanding of object formation and on action knowledge preceding object knowledge.

The first forms of symbols in children are found in imitative gestures and pretend play. In this connection the conceptual difficulty about the construction of an object is no longer so pressing; it is relatively easy to admit that children construct symbols at play. However, at this point a specific observation can be made concerning a good part of symbolic acts: it requires a motivation over and beyond the present action. To recognize this piece of furniture as a chair when you are intent on sitting down on it requires no other motivation besides the one that is included in your present action. No explanation is needed why you perceive this thing as a chair; the thing is a chair. But if this chair brings to your mind an unpleasant association in connection with your personal life, or if someone daydreams about a beach-chair or produces doodles in the shape of a chair, the question of *why?* becomes pertinent. Clearly there are some symbolic actions for which answers to the *why?* seem as obvious as to nonsymbolic actions. For instance, to call somebody to the table when the meal is ready or to produce the portrait of somebody who pays you for the service requires no more complicated reason than explaining why you cook a meal when you are hungry or why you work for money. However, as soon as we get away from direct means-end situations and consider such symbolic acts as free mental associations, dreams, or pretend playing, no explanation of symbol production is complete that does not include some answer to the *why*.

At this point Freud's contribution to our understanding of symbols looms large. Not only was he the pioneer who discovered the common symbolic nature underlying a variety of acts (such as dreams, jokes, misplaced actions) that were not systematically recognized as such. More important, he provided a model of dynamic relations between drive and symbol in postulating drive impulses as the motivating force for symbolic acts. And Freud charted the personal history of these impulses, starting in infancy, not unlike Piaget, who explained a present state of knowledge in terms of its individual acquisition.

FREUD AND PIAGET

Here then is the point where Piaget and Freud meet. While Piaget explained the *how* of actions and symbols, their internal organization and logical cohesiveness, Freud explored the *why* behind these acts and the dynamic economy within the household of personal impulses and drives. On the surface they seemed to be miles apart: Piaget starting from the philosophical premise of logical universals, searching for their implicit beginnings in biological action and organization; Freud, avoiding philosophical perspectives and conscious logic, probing for the "honest" reasons behind ostensibly rational and irrational actions; the former as uncomfortable with emotional imbalance and subjective diversity as the latter was suspicious of rational balance ("rationalization"). This contrast, if not opposition, is reinforced by the simplistic stereotype that for Freud everything is ultimately related to the unruly sex drive, while for Piaget all behavior, from the most primitive biological level to the highest reaches of human reasoning, can be formalized in the language of logical composition.

If these clichès are understood in the reductionist sense of "all is sex" or "all is logic," then indeed there is no common ground between these two psychologists. But only someone determined to reject their theories out of hand would interpret them in this way. In reality what they are saying is almost the opposite; namely, that there is an implicit sexual drive component and an implicit logical reason component in any action, but no human action is (or can be) merely one or the other.

To a sympathetic interpreter of their works—and here sympathetic does not mean at all mindlessly following the leader, rather it stands for a critical attitude that searches for what is primary in their respective research programs—the two scholars have a lot in common, both in their work and their personal habits. In spite of appearances to the contrary, they were both modest in their theoretical claims, willing to criticize and change their views and say so openly. They worked systematically in a one-step-after-the-other fashion and kept close to empirical observations. Neither envisaged a complete science of psychology; each had his favorite alibi for avoiding sweeping statements or complete solutions. Freud referred to his ultimate interest in clinical cases where every action is overdetermined (with no definite limit), and Piaget referred to his focus on logical knowledge with neglect of emotions and individual differences ($4 + 7 = 11$ regardless of a person's emotional state or the particular culture). Both were highly disciplined and wrote habitually day after day. Their literary output is quite similar in sheer bulk of books and articles. That Freud over and above his scholarly interest was a superb writer with an easy style contributed no doubt to the spread of his theory. Unfortunately this cannot be said for Piaget—but then is it possible to combine epistemological depth with literary style?

To turn now to the work itself, first it should be emphasized that both scholars had biological training and shared the conviction that biological principles were operating in human life. Freud once remarked that reason had been exalted all too prominently by the sages of the past and his task was to remind us that human psychology is still driven by biological impulses. Initially Freud attempted to link these impulses directly to bodily processes; but quite soon he abandoned this direct physiological perspective.

While retaining the concept of drive, he treated it more and more as a psychological given that was influencing and was being influenced by the history of each individual. It is unfortunate that the English translation of Freud's word for drive *(Trieb)* is "instinct." Instinct, properly speaking, means an innate action pattern, such as nest building, mating, defense of territory, and as such is closer to the *how* than to the *why* of an action. Typically, instinctual actions are similar in all individuals of a species and have been so for thousands of generations. Drive, on the other hand, is a fitting word for the energy aspect underlying biological actions. In humans the connection between drive and action is not at all rigid so as to result in similar instinctual actions. On the contrary, Freud showed how the drive itself undergoes changes and that the potential actions energized by the drive are literally limitless and change as a function of culture and personality.

While Freud in this manner "psychologized" biological drives and extended them to the outer reaches of human achievement, Piaget in a fashion "biologized" logical reason and traced its origin to the most primitive living organization. He too, like Freud, tended to exaggerate his key perspective in several attempts to express this organization in formalized logical language. But ultimately his major contributions and concepts were firmly rooted in psychology. Both Freud and Piaget were marvelous observers of human behavior and achieved originality and depth of interpretation not the least because they had a common commitment to find reason in acts that others considered irrational or just trivial. While his contemporaries considered dreams or mental disorders a weakness of the brain or the nerves *and left it at that*—hence the word *neurosis*—Freud searched for their psychological causes. Similarly, philosophers extensively and variously linked the uniqueness of human knowledge to the power of language and symbols *and left it at that*, but Piaget searched for the source of this power and found it in human development. Thus, coming from quite different directions, both scholars focused on the growing child to provide the key to the specificity of human emotions as well as to the universality of logical reason.

At this point the reader may well be persuaded that both Piaget and Freud made significant contributions to our understanding of the child by describing the psychology and the development of knowledge and emotions. There are a number of scholars sympathetic to both Freud and Piaget who have set out to make comparisons between them. In the main these comparisons have taken the form of setting Piaget's stages of knowledge against Freud's stages of drive development. These studies are certainly useful and have some empirical value. My goal in this work, however, is quite different. I am not after an external comparison that will leave emotions and knowledge as separate as they were in the beginning. Rather I aim at an internal integration so that emotions and knowledge are no longer neatly divided as two different psychological compartments.

To accomplish this I shall first focus on object knowledge and symbol formation as described by Piaget (chapter 2). Armed with this theoretical framework, I will attempt to reinterpret Freud's basic position on the dynamics of unconscious symbol formation within Piaget's developmental model (chapter 3). From this should follow a more general integration of the two theories based on their main concepts and core research programs. That is, a perspective should evolve in which emotions and knowledge can be treated in a unified manner, whether the behavior in question is the symbolic play of children or theory building in mathematics (chapter 4). The developmental approach to emotions and knowledge will then be extended to a larger biological scale; evolutionary considerations of humanization will be related to object knowledge and symbol formation (chapter 5). But then, if emotions and knowledge are developmentally linked, how is it possible to have logically necessary categories that are socially universal and individually normative (chapter 6)? A short epilogue, in place of a summing-up, will explicate Piaget's claim that logic is indeed a morality of thought and that as a consequence all human knowledge belongs to the context for which evolution has selected the human animal: the context of interpersonal relations (chapter 7).

2.

The Formation
of the Symbolic World

IN THIS CHAPTER I will draw on Piaget's early research in which he systematically observed the actions of his own three children during their first years of life. This work was published as a trilogy: *The Origins of Intelligence, The Construction of Reality,* and *Symbol Formation.* While the second book deals basically with the formation of the object, the English translation of the third book has as its title a portion of the original subtitle, *Play, Dreams, and Imitation*— a not so subtle indication that English-speaking readers are not likely to be attracted by the question of object- and symbol-formation. But the formation of knowledge is what Piaget's work is all about. The concepts of object and symbol are the elements upon which his further theory of operations and equilibration is based. Without this grounding an adequate comprehension of the theory is improbable. Note especially the words *construction* and *formation.* They spell out Piaget's research strategy. Rejecting the two extremes of innatism (given by heredity) and environmentalism (learned from outside experience), Piaget looked for a third source from which knowledge arises. This he found in the constructive activities of the developing child, starting with the most primitive reflex actions of the newborn infant.

The word *knowledge* is far from having a clear and definite meaning in everyday language, just like the word *symbol* discussed earlier. Some scholars would like to limit its use to a particular form, namely, scientific knowledge, or at the least, to theoretical knowledge that is articulated, shared with others and confirmed by actual events ("objective" knowledge). Obviously young children do not have this kind of knowledge. Yet it is present in all healthy adults. Philosophers have inquired into the nature of adult objective knowledge and in this connection proposed various epistemological theories. Piaget, equally intent on this issue, took his cue from the knowledge observed in children. So instead of asking, what is the nature of knowledge (leading invariably to answers based primarily on philosophical speculations), he probed the question how an infant's knowledge changes into adult knowledge, a question that is basically amenable to empirical observation and control. This kind of causal-historical perspective, in fact, helped to originate modern Western science. So in this respect Piaget followed a hallowed and proven tradition.

Admittedly to frame a question about the genesis of knowledge presupposes that there is in fact a genesis, that is, the coming into being of something new. As a biologist, Piaget was familiar with biological transformations in individual and evolutionary development. He considered the change from a knowledge state A to a knowledge state B from the perspective of biological transformation. On the one hand there is novelty and thus discontinuity between A and B. But at the same time there also must be continuity, an invariance from A to B, otherwise this would not be a biological transformation but a metaphysical transmutation. These biological considerations led Piaget to extend the usual meaning of knowledge to human infants and beyond, into the realm of general biological adaptation.

If adaptation means the sum total of organism-environment regulations, specific to each biological species, can one not conceive of human knowledge in a similar manner? Yet there is an obvious contrast. The overwhelming majority of regulations in subhuman species are acquired in evolution; they are preformed at birth or rigidly channeled through maturation with only a limited degree of freedom. The regulations of human knowledge, however, are not only not pre-formed at birth, they become the means of infinite openness and creative newness. As a consequence the relatively rigid organism-environment connection is burst asunder and poses the major problem for any theory of knowledge. The reality to which human knowledge is adapted is not a fixed entity; whatever it is—and we shall come back to this question in chapter 5—it is a constantly and increasingly changing world corresponding to the openness of human knowledge.

But is there a common link between these vastly different regulations of instinctual and of adult knowledge? Four commonalities can be listed: they regulate actions on the environment; they are acquired in phylogeny (evolution) or ontogeny (individual development) as a function of these actions; they imply more than passive reactions to environmental pressure, hence the complementary processes of assimilation and accommodation; finally these regulations have logical-mathematical properties and can be suitably expressed in logical-mathematical language. This last commonality is Piaget's original contribution, and on the strength of this he did not hesitate to endow even the most primitive organism with some form of knowledge.

Wherever there is life there is logic, could be called Piaget's fundamental position on knowledge. The reverse is equally true: all logic is primarily related to life, action and assimilation. This position, moreover, points a way out of several problems facing anyone seriously concerned with human knowledge. One is the relation between knowledge in its ordinary meaning— consciously articulated logical knowledge—and knowledge in other contexts, such as covert and implicit forms of knowledge. Another problem is that knowledge, as an entity in itself, is not something readily circumscribed. It is real, of course, but it is not a physical thing, rather it has a psychological-biological reality that is, moreover, not so much in the organism by itself but in relation to its action on the environment. It is an active (i.e., living) relation between an agent and an object of action and it relates a knower (a subject) and an object of knowledge. But, Piaget insists, this relation—whatever the specific organism and the specific context—has a logical structure.

This structural characteristic gave Piaget the key to the—originally philosophical—problem of knowledge. For now Piaget could specify both what was continuous and what was discontinuous in human knowledge development. A logical structure as such (what he called the "logical function") is one of the four invariants mentioned above, but what is changing in development is the form of the logical structures. There are qualitative differences between what Piaget calls different stages of knowing. In sum, Piaget postulated that logical structures are constitutive both of knowledge in general and of different stages of knowledge specifically.

To comprehend Piaget's use of the concept of knowledge, consider first a typical biologically determined action. Your digestive system "knows" how to deal with food intake, breaking it down into chemical components that can be assimilated to various vital functions. Never mind that this chemical process is not your personal achievement, that it belongs to you as a species, not as an individual. Clearly the chemical formulas that express its function have logical-mathematical properties. Then observe the action of a seven-year-old girl jumping over the rope she is swinging over her head, front, down, back, up. This action implies an extensive know-how of body position and movement, of rotating the rope around the hip axis, of holding it at the right length, and of timing. All these aspects could be expressed in precise logical-mathematical language, if the need or the occasion for it arose (such as for purposes of movement training or computer simulation). In both cases we observe a temporal and spatial coordination of different inputs and different capabilities. And coordination always implies a logical-mathematical structure in accordance with which there is ordering, classifying, relating different means to a common end.

Based on this biological perspective, Piaget was concerned with knowledge insofar as it is the general coordination of an action, that is, the general *form* of the knowledge, not its particular *content*. Another way of saying the same is to define knowledge as the general organization of an action, keeping in mind that organization derives from organism. Human psychology has for Piaget two aspects, knowledge (or cognition), which is our concern here, and the dynamic or motivational aspect for which we shall turn to Freud. Yet even from what has been said so far, it is clear that any sort of neat separation between the two is out of the question, all the more so as Piaget constantly stressed the action orientation of knowledge and the autonomous character of the regulations.

However, you may contend, scientific or theoretical knowledge is not an action; on the contrary it is something that is present to us apart from action. Indeed, if knowledge is at all linked to action, it is customary to think of it as something that comes first, knowledge before action. The examples given so far were knowledge in action, and for that reason their designation as knowledge is controversial. To overcome this conceptual hurdle, you can add the word "internal" or "possible" to Piaget's definition of knowledge: knowledge is the general coordination of a present ("real") or possible ("internal") action. There you have an all encompassing phrase. It covers knowledge from biological digestion to sensorimotor jump rope to theoretical physics.

Reflect how the recent insights of theoretical physics have changed the concrete reality of our world. Even though our knowledge can become intentionally disconnected from a present action, it can never be unrelated to action. Just as perception is an action (as pointed out in chapter 1), as when a two-year-old toddler takes on the challenge of a staircase, it too can become intentionally disconnected from a present action. But a possible action is always implied. To see a staircase on the other side of the square implies the possibility of going over there and using it to reach a higher level or doing something else relative to the staircase.

Precisely because human knowledge can take the form of a possible (not present) action, the inquiry of what this theoretical knowledge is and how it comes to be would seem to be the most natural thing on earth. Actually this is far from being the case. In fact, our psychological capabilities as they are directed to our habitual way of life have always appeared to us simply as given, normative, natural. It requires a heroic effort to take a point of view different from our own subjective selves, our own culture, social milieu, or other present historical contingencies. This is too well known to require any documentation except to point out there there is no final absolute knowledge that can overcome all subjective viewpoints; rather, "unbiased" knowledge is an ideal toward which we can strive but can never reach.

Leaving this perennial problem of the relativity of knowledge aside—notwithstanding the universality of logical-mathematical operations which Piaget vigorously defends—the mystery of what kind of knowledge there is in infants can only be approached if we stop projecting our way of theoretical knowing into the actions of the infants. Two reasons militate against seeing the world from the viewpoint of the other, emotional resistance and a limited point of view. Only the second factor is pertinent in the present discussion.

When knowledge is *a priori* limited to the theoretical knowledge of developed adults, there remain only two choices vis-à-vis infants: either they are assumed to be bereft of knowledge or, at the other extreme, knowledge is considered innate, but its expression in infants is blocked by extraneous circumstances. In the latter case, infants are assumed to have perception, learning, reasoning, intention, memory, images, pretty much as those phenomena are observed in adults. Proponents of this theory often criticize Piaget for underestimating the knowledge capacities of infants. In either case our understanding of knowledge remains adult-centered and a study of infants cannot contribute to its better understanding. The question of knowledge is not really dealt with; at best, we learn whether or not adult knowledge is found in a certain population.

In contrast Piaget approached the problem of knowledge both as a biologist and as a philosopher. His philosophical background made him sensitive to many serious problems that philosophers had raised about human knowledge, such as, what is an object of knowledge, what is objective knowledge, how can logic and mathematics be necessary or universal and yet correspond so marvelously to individual object experience, above all, can there be new knowledge or is new knowledge merely the discovery of something that has been there all along but not been found previously? To all these questions about knowledge, Piaget was convinced, there was an answer that was more than adult-centered philosophical speculation. This could be done if the philosophical form of asking the question, *what is it?* is turned into an observable, empirical form: *how does it come to be?*

This empirical perspective afforded Piaget the opportunity to observe in systematic fashion how infants at first construct a logic of action that gradually leads to the formation of the permanent object. Object knowledge and its corollary symbol formation in turn have three monumental consequences that will engage us throughout this essay. First, they change the world from a present action universe to the limitless openness of symbolic possibilities; second, they create the need and are the precondition for a coordination of necessary logic and universal categories; third, they transform the undifferentiated dependency relation of infancy into an interpersonal relation based on the recognition of *you* as an *other-than-I*. The last two transformations will take a long time, namely the period of ten to twenty years during which the toddler psychologically grows into a young adult. The first transformation from the present action universe to a symbolic universe has a more immediate impact and is the proper focus of this and the two subsequent chapters.

OBJECT-FORMATION

What precisely does Piaget mean when he postulates that new-born infants live in a psychological reality without objects? He asserts that they do not face the universe as we adults do. We are aware of ourselves living in a world of stable dimensions of space, time, causality; we know the universe as a totality of relatively permanent objects and ourselves as part of it. Piaget considered this kind of object awareness the end point of a gradual knowledge development that needs to be explored. Here can be noticed Piaget's consistent research strategy. He observes a particular knowledge form, namely object knowledge, universally present in adult theoretical knowledge, and rather than accepting it as a given, he asks the biologist's questions: what is its function? how does it come to be? It is apparent that without a serious study of philosophical questions into the nature of knowledge it would never have occurred to Piaget to explore the status of object knowledge. These two theoretical perspectives, biological and philosophical, were necessary preliminaries, but a third, empirical factor had to be added. How can you observe something that is nothing short of a difficult philosophical concept and, moreover, do this in infancy before mastery of language? This third factor is perhaps Piaget's most notable gift and shows his creativity at its most obvious.

Object of knowledge is indeed an awesomely theoretical concept, and readers will look in vain in Piaget's writing for abstract definitions and discussions. Piaget avoided these for good reasons. He did not want to lose himself in philosophical speculations, notwithstanding his use of philosophical insights in the service of an empirical inquiry into the development of knowledge. Freud too used the concept of *object,* but like Piaget avoided premature and lengthy abstract discussion of theoretical concepts. He, like Piaget, used these concepts to serve his quest for understanding psychological reality and not the other way around. This attitude marked both scholars as great psychologists. In the case of *object*—a purely abstract concept—Piaget spoke of "the permanent object," or more precisely, "the permanent object of an action," and with this simple transformation a difficult philosophical notion became amenable to the observation of anyone interested in infants' actions. To state it at once, the permanent object is the crucial ingredient of the out-of-sight-out-of-mind situation, of any peek-a-boo or hide-and-seek game.

You cannot observe knowledge directly, but you can observe action. Every action is a coordination of environmental input and the organizer's capabilities; this coordination *is* the knowledge underlying the action. As Piaget observed the first actions of his children, it became clear to him that the early sucking or grasping reflexes in no way implied an active coordination with an object, rather the object was passively present and merely activated the reflex action. The infant did not act on an object even though the object occasioned the action. This distinction is crucial; it is the distinction between a physical and a psychological contact. This has nothing to do with consciousness, but everything with assimilation.

Infants from the start engage in an active assimilatory function (the only thing that is, strictly speaking, innate, Piaget admits) but there is no object or subject as yet. Knowledge involving object and subject will evolve in a sequential fashion through the elaboration of this assimilatory function. The evidence for this statement is the initial absence, and—since absence alone is never sufficient—the systematically increasing scope of locating and searching for a present object-of-action. When the object becomes "permanent" in the absence of a present action, it can be said that the object-of-action has become an object-of-knowledge. Even within the period of a few days after birth, the infants' active orientations toward the nipple, the focusing of their eyes on an interesting sight, the grabbing of a particular thing, dramatically improve, and these are the easily observable beginnings of something that was absent at birth and will continue to develop into the permanent object.

Object knowledge is therefore a knowledge achievement resulting from the infant's actions, and it is, to start with, limited to something-to-act-on in present action. In other words, between the initial state of a universe without objects and the final state of a universe of permanent objects-of-knowledge, there is the elaboration of a universe of objects-of-action. These achievements are motivated by momentary functional needs. Take the active effort of regaining a displaced object, such as the nipple. This action of compensating for a felt deficiency (interruption of sucking) is at the same time the constructing of something new: an object-to-assimilate.

The first objects-of-actions, characteristic of substage 1, are far from stable, they are but the first glimmer of an object construction that will continue for the next two years. Nevertheless, compared to the initial state of biological reflex activity, there is newness in having an object-to-assimilate, albeit only in a fleeting and momentary fashion. That means the baby will make some small directed movements toward the nipple or will focus the vision on a sight for a few seconds, nothing more. If the object is too far away or there is the slightest distraction, the object of the action disappears to the baby's psychology and cannot be retrieved. Clearly the object has no independent (i.e., permanent) existence; it is but an extension of the child's assimilation.

Hand in hand with the dawn of the object-of-assimilation is an even more rudimentary form of the complementary function of knowledge, namely accommodation. An action of sucking, momentarily interrupted, occasions some dim awareness of the action in order to regulate the interruption and to adjust to the concrete situation. Just as the regulation of the action leads to an improved assimilatory function (recognition of an object-to-assimilate), the adjustment foreshadows the accommodatory function. However, at this stage it is almost too early to speak of accommodation since accommodation needs an object to which to accommodate.

Objects become more solid in the next stage, substage 2, when infants engage in repetitive bodily actions (hand, feet, or facial movements, thumb sucking). This is the first clear separation of assimilation and accommodation. Take as an illustration an interesting sight connected with a movement. The sight could be the infant's own hands—not known as "my hands"—and the movement a circular moving of the hands in front of the eyes. This indicates an interconnection of assimilatory schemes, namely, schemes of vision and schemes of movement are both directed at the same object, and this interconnection solidifies the universe of action. If during this action the baby's head would fall sideways, the baby could accommodate the action so as to continue the movement in front of the eyes, just as the baby can suck the thumb in different bodily positions. But as yet there is no active search, only a slight adjustment of an ongoing accommodation. When this does not succeed it is still "out of sight, out of mind."

In contrast, around six months, there is something that looks like a search for an object. But Piaget points out that in substage 3 the removal of an obstacle covering an interesting sight indicates less an interest in the object than the freeing of the child's interrupted activity. Active search begins about three months later in substage 4. Now for the first time, one is justified in assuming that the children know something about objects being situated in space. When you hide an object behind two screens, the infants will not give up after failing to find it behind the first screen but will remove the second. This is evidence for an active search, but it will be seen that even at this stage the object is still closely connected to the action and has not yet a solid independent existence.

The experiment just described can be continued after the infant finds the object behind screen A. The object is taken from the infant and in full view of the attentive infant is hidden behind screen B. In this situation infants will invariably look first behind screen A, repeating the action that brought success before. It is as if they trusted their own action-memory more than their present visual spatial perception. How else is it possible that they repeat an action that is perceptibly in the wrong place? Now if the object, as Piaget postulates, is gradually constructed from a state of initial undifferentiation as part of the assimilatory action, it follows that infants recognize their own actions before they recognize the object as action-independent. In this case they have reached the stage where they can search for the object through a successful action, but once having succeeded, they fail to switch. They behave as if the object owed its existence to that particular action.

This experiment has been replicated many times under more controlled conditions, such as videotaping the infants' eyes to make sure they pay attention to where the object is being hidden. An ingenious modification was hiding the object under a transparent plastic cover. The object was not really hidden from sight, it was merely out of reach. And what do infants do at that stage of object development? They do exactly as above: having succeeded to grab the object after removal of cover A, they go back to cover A even though their eyes are still glued to cover B, under which they see the object they want to retrieve.

What inferences can be made from these observations about the universe of infants around one year of age? On the positive side, they have achieved a certain solidification of the action-object, and in ordinary circumstances this object is regarded as external to the action. This accomplishment is due to the increasingly complex intercoordination—Piaget calls it mutual assimilation—of knowledge schemes. The evolutionary important hand-eye coordination is conspicuous at this age; vision and hand and body movement interact to keep an interesting object in midline at a suitable distance to be explored both visually and manually. Scheme coordination focuses on the assimilatory function of knowledge. To "understand" an object means to assimilate it to an increasingly complex and logically and hierarchically ordered network of schemes.

Children now understand the difference between their own hand as part of their action and another's hand as the object of the action of grabbing. In the example the infants coordinate their schemes of vision (things look different from different perspectives), handling and body orientation in the one common action on the object. The coordination of schemes gives the objects meaning and a certain degree of permanent substance. Note that schemes are instruments of assimilation, nothing else; the phrase *assimilatory schemes* is really redundant, there are no other sort of schemes.

Equally important at this stage is the accommodatory function of knowledge that is outward directed and is increasingly reinforced by the specific concrete features of the object. At earlier stages the infants' interests seemed to be confined to their own actions and feeling states; objects were experienced more as extensions of their assimilatory actions rather than in their own right. Now there is a remarkable opening up to the world "outside," and objects as such become the center of interest. To accommodate means to adjust knowledge schemes to a particular situation, more precisely, to some newness, some unexpected challenging resistance in the object. This is the beginning of the human love affair with the world of objects. Accommodation becomes the challenging occasion to use and to enrich the content of available schemes. Compared to the solipsism of earlier stages, this construction of a universe of action-objects is a veritable revolution. It is indicated most dramatically in intentional means-end actions. Children will now remove obstacles or they will pull or push things to reach a desired end. Intentional (i.e., active) accommodations of schemes to the objects of actions contribute to the gradual separation of objects and actions, a precondition for the eventual externalization and objectivation of the universe.

It is typical of knowledge development that any improvement is at the same time the occasion for a knowledge disturbance, which in turn will lead to its compensation and further improvement. The infants who for the first time have mastered a primitive form of object knowledge are in no position to know the limits of their fragile knowledge. They know to remove an obstacle to get to something out of reach. This knowledge is practically useful and, if it is successful once, it is usually successful a second time. But in the hiding experiment described above, the usual routine is broken and the object is hidden in a different location. The children's attempt to find it again in the first location indicate the weakness of their object knowledge.

For us every object is linked to a stable system of spatial and temporal understanding as well as to physical causality. These three know-hows are intimately linked with each other and with object knowledge. For the infant the object is principally experienced as a result of a particular action, not as existing within an independent spatial and temporal system. Here we can observe the sensorimotor origin of magical thinking which will later mushroom and extend far beyond infancy. The basic formula of magical thinking is: "my" action causes a certain object (event) to be. This is precisely what infants who have achieved means-end object knowledge constantly experience. The universe appears to them to be at the beck and call of their actions. They have learned that objects are the results of their actions; from now on they have to unlearn or, more precisely, to learn the realistic limits of their own actions. Continuing contact with people and things will provide the necessary resistances and occasions for knowledge disturbances and favor this further development. But this is no passive imposition from outside. Only their own active restructuring of their schemes—Piaget's equilibration—can lead infants out of the magic of their action world, as in subsequent years it will lead the symbolizing children out of the magic of their symbol world.

Infants by one year of age are able to recognize certain objective features of the environment, such as their parents in contrast to other familiar or unfamiliar adults, who at times may elicit fear and avoidance responses. Does this not indicate that they have developed object knowledge, at least in the sense of differentiating between similar objects? Not at all. We have to be careful and analyze our use of words. For *adults* to recognize someone usually implies that they are aware of encountering a person whom they have met in the past. Moreover, this awareness is prior to any present action in which they may engage the person. This form of recognitory awareness is therefore an action-separated knowledge or, as it was called earlier, theoretical knowledge. It is therefore psychologically linked to a theoretical knowledge of the past and to a multitude of general and specific knowledges available at the moment.

As was said at the beginning of this chapter, if it is not possible to imagine any other way of memory recognition, it is necessary to postulate all these theoretical knowledges as operating in one-year-old children. Specifically, and in accord with an adult's experience of being able to form an image or representation of absent situations, infants too would have to be equipped with mental representations or images of things they recognize. The mental image becomes the causal antecedent that "explains" recognition. Hence the necessary inference: recognitory memory is evidence for the presence of a mental image.

This line of reasoning assumes theoretical knowledge as primary and as a given. In contrast, Piaget's theory of knowledge takes the standpoint of biological action as primary and explains theoretical knowledge as the achievement of sequential developmental stages. Therefore the theory has no need to populate infantile minds with internal images to enable them to learn, to discriminate, to recognize. All these feats are accomplished within the action schemes (i.e., action know-hows) as they are being used in their proper business of assimilation. All assimilation can be said to be a form of recognition, a recognizing of a reciprocity or similarity ("as-similation") between environment and organism. If internal images are preconditions of recognition, at what point in biology would we introduce them? Do cows carry around internal images of edible grass to allow them to discriminate and recognize a luscious pasture from less satisfying ground? Assimilation at all times implies an environment-organism exchange, an action of the organism to effect a change in the environment. At biological levels the environmental object is entirely centered on the assimilating organism. This is still true for the psychology of human infants in their first year. The four-months-old baby girl who smiles contentedly at her mother is assimilating the situation to her scheme of contentment. This is a present bodily attitude (or feeling) of mutual conformity between scheme and object. If we must use the words "recognition memory" we should realize that what the subject recognizes is her own action, long before she knows mother as an object.

The permanent object is knowledge of a physical event, enclosed in a system of spatial and temporal dimensions and of physical causality. "Permanent" means here independence from the subject's own action. We have witnessed a certain degree of permanence in the object of a one-year-old child's action, most conspicuously in means-end relations where instrumental actions are employed to obtain an absent (hidden) object. Around this time the infant turns into a highly mobile toddler. With standing up and walking comes a qualitative shift in actively exploring space and observing objects. The newly achieved opening up to the world of objects is now constantly enlarged as toddlers search out the world of action available to them. In this reaching out they are attracted by an endless array of new and challenging situations.

These explorations, typical of substage 5, are at times quite systematic and take on something of the character of a scientific experiment. Dropping things has been a favorite occupation of the little ones for some time; but at first the interest was merely centered on the action, as if the infant said to the world: "I know how to drop things, I can make things fall and go boom." No attention was given to the object dropped, in fact, the infant frequently seemed to search for it momentarily, but not finding it immediately the search is quickly abandoned. Some six months later, say at one year and two months, toddlers are still observed to drop things, but there is a dramatic difference in three respects. First, the attention is on the object or, better, the result of the action and second, the toddler knows how to retrieve it even if it should accidentally roll behind or under some visual obstacle. Third, the action is not repeated in a haphazard routine manner, as previously in "circular reactions" to bring about the same desired result, but at times the children go about it in an explorative systematic manner, indicating an implicit intention to learn something about the object, the physical act of falling, or some other spatial relation.

In these early explorations it is possible to indicate the three criteria a "scientific" object should satisfy: it should permit anticipation, it should permit control and experimentation, and it should be part of a systematic totality. Anticipation is observed as children look in the direction of the falling object as compared to the aimless looking around a few months earlier. Similarly, as the children reach out to hold something in their hand, they now accommodate the fingers to the features of the object before, not merely after, physical contact. The evidence for control and experimentation is provided by the systematic variations in their actions which seem to pose a question to the world, such as, where will the object fall if I drop it from different heights or with different degrees of push or, which different actions are going to be successful in reaching an intended result?

Finally, the interconnections of spatial, temporal, and causal relations relative to the actions of a subject, insofar as they are experienced and coordinated in action, lead to the construction of the permanent object (substage 6). This object, it should be clear by now, is not a thing or one particular object, rather it is a quality of knowing the world of actions and ushers in the world of known objects. When I referred to the systematic "scientific" exploration of toddlers, the object concept (in the process of being constructed) can be called the general system within which the actions are done. It is the totality of relations, elaborated through personal activity, between the various objects-of-action. Piaget observed the object's final construction around 18 months of age in the systematic search for things that were hidden and were further displaced while being hidden. In other words, here was a true hide-and-seek game with no other cues than the systematic knowledge that, unless physically removed, things continue to exist permanently in space and time.

It is helpful to think of the object concept as part of the sensorimotor action world in which one- to two-year-old children live. It is the logical framework that provides permanence, stability, "objectivity" to their present actions. The universe is no longer a shifting sequence of momentary impressions centered on the assimilation of the universe to the self—which does not know that is is a self. Now children know, in action not in thought, that as a rule, actions have the expected results; that there are objects (things and people) that exist outside of their actions, to whom they can relate through these actions (and vice versa); that they themselves and their actions are part of this object world. If knowledge as exemplified in physiological processes or instinctual action patterns indicates a biological logic or intellegence of the organism, the sensorimotor knowledge of the 18-month-old child is proof of a logic and intelligence of actions. Piaget called it sensorimotor intelligence.

From the viewpoint of a theory of knowledge, the two characteristics of sensorimotor knowledge are: first, it is not innate, that is, it is the direct product of individual experience (developmental experience); second, it is not (theoretical) thought but present action. I add that the first point carries, if not a logical, at least a biological necessity. The open-ended variations of possible actions, corresponding to the unlimited variety of objects-of-actions, imply a degree of individual freedom that cannot be present in the logic of innate knowledge but precisely requires the logic of developmental knowledge. The second point follows from the first. Action knowledge must first be constituted in its own right as the relation of agent-action-object before it is separated from the action component as a subject-object relation.

The development of the logic of the permanent object—also called by Piaget the conservation of the object—has revolutionized the action universe of infancy in a generally uninterrupted progress. The young child's action knowledge appears relatively realistic, successful, and stable. Not that there is no further progress in the understanding of the action world. Far from it. What Piaget implies is that the logic of action has reached a certain closure in the permanent object, and that further logical development is in the direction of the object as such rather than in the action on the object. As an illustration of this statement, consider this two-year-old boy seeing his father standing on top of a dam. The boy makes a beeline toward him without adjusting the path or his body position to the steepness of the incline; in other words, he assimilates the situation to his habitual, sensori-motor walking scheme—and falls. A year later the boy is observed in a similar situation and without hesitation he adopts a realistic strategy of going up in diagonal fashion. This improvement is probably due to repeated exposure to walking and balancing in different terrains and does not require anything new in the general logic of action, certainly not any theoretical knowledge of angle of the diagonal to the incline.

SYMBOL-FORMATION

So where does one look for the psychological conse-quences of object-formation? Now finally we come to the crucial concept of symbol, briefly discussed in the previous chapter. My proposition is this: object formation is the prerequisite of symbol formation, and any explanation of the symbol must include an understanding of the object concept. First, however, keep in mind that object and symbol are not parallel notions and do not lie on the same reality plane. Object, as a general concept, refers to a logical frame of knowledge, symbol to a specific type of action made possible by object knowledge. Object knowledge implies the separation of the object of knowledge (whatever the object may be in a specific case) from the subject's action. During the senso-rimotor period, there is the development of knowledge-in-action;

in due course this development leads to a certain closure in the form of the permanent object. The object of action becomes an object of knowledge. With this transformation knowledge can be detached from the action and takes on a life of its own. Henceforth it can function in two different action types: first, in the form of knowledge-as-action (corresponding to the previous knowledge-in-action), as for instance in the systematic search of the hide and seek situation; and second, in the form of knowledge-as-symbol, which for the child is an altogether new psychological experience.

Symbol-formation is then the most dramatic consequence of object-formation. Children around age two are entering into a new psychological reality, the world of symbols is added to the world of actions. Different forms of symbols have been surveyed in chapter 1, and I merely list them here again in order to make it easier to picture what is really new in the psychology of these children: imitation in the absence of the model, recall memory, pretend play, speech-in-communication, speech-for-self (internal speech), fantasy, internal images, imagination, dreams. This is indeed a vast array of different acts, which Piaget was the first to clearly recognize as having a common psychological origin. At first he referred to them collectively as the symbolic function; later when he felt the need to limit the meaning of symbols, he called it the semiotic function. I have suggested that *symbolic function* be used, not least because *semiotic* is a highly technical term and has no form corresponding to "symbol" or "symbolize," but also because the distinction Piaget wanted to make between "motivated" symbols and "conventional" signs is not as clear as it may seem.

Piaget explains symbol-formation in terms of his action theory of sensorimotor development. Its sources are both in the assimilatory and in the accommodatory function of knowing. For reasons that will become clear later on, he focused on pretend play as the most obvious and easily observable symbolic behavior. A three-year-old child playing car uses a small piece of wood, moving it around the floor under, over, and in-between various pieces of furniture, all the time accompanying the movement with an audible roar that gets louder as the movement gets faster and with an exclamation of "crash" when the wood strikes a solid obstacle. Here is a clear symbolic action; the playing as a whole is the symbol, and the meaning of the symbol is beyond the observable action. Where is it to be found? One obvious suggestion would be: a real car as it moves along, probably the family car.

However, on the basis of the present discussion, we can be much more precise—both from a philosophical as well as a psychological perspective. The meaning of the play indeed is the car, but only insofar as the car is an object-of-knowledge. In short, the play signifies not the car as a physical thing but the car as an object. What is this object, and where is it? We know the answer. Object of the car means the car-known-as-an object, and this knowledge is constructed by the child who is playing. You may ask, did not this child know what a car is much earlier? Certainly a one-year-old child in our culture may know the function of a car, but this is sensorimotor knowledge-in-action, a knowledge attached to the present state of being (or wanting to be) in contact with the car. Insofar as in symbol-formation knowledge is detached from the action, sensorimotor acquaintance is not adequate for the symbolic function.

I have so far stressed the newness of the symbolic function, precisely because its special construction has generally been neglected or it is simply taken for granted without any further explanation. However, a developmental newness must not be exaggerated and turned into a caricature. The two-year-old child does not wake up one day and exclaim: "Hurrah, I am living in a symbolic world." All changes in development are gradual and take time. It took the best part of two years to construct a relatively stable action world. It will take twice as much before children around age six can adequately recognize the symbolic world and distinguish it from the action world, and another eight to ten years before they have the appropriate logical framework to regulate symbolic reality. Therefore, just as the object concept is gradually constructed until the attainment of closure and independence in the formation of the permanent object, likewise symbolic play and symbolic objects have forerunners that anticipate in part the functions of the final developmental product. In general, Piaget derives play action from the assimilatory, and symbolic objects from the accommodatory function.

Sensorimotor accommodation invariably involves an imitation component. The grasp of holding a ball differs from the grasp of holding a stick, a visual focusing on a face differs from a focusing on a table. In each instance the accommodation of the respective schemes of assimilation "imitates" the outline of the thing assimilated. In conjunction with infants' assimilatory activity ("to grasp," "to look at"), accommodatory imitation provides a first contact with things "out there" even though they are still unaware of the boundary between the outside and their own actions.

> It is not that a perception begins by being interesting or meaningful and later acquires a motor power through association with a movement: it is interesting or meaningful just because it intervenes in the performance of an action and is thus assimilated to a sensorimotor scheme. The first datum is therefore neither the perception, nor the movement, nor the association of the two, but the assimilation of the perceived object to a scheme of action, which is at the same time motor reproduction and perceptive recognition, i.e., reproductive and recognitive assimilation. (1937:17)

Piaget goes on to say that assimilation provides both meaning and the motivation to repeat the action in circular fashion. During these early stages, accommodation decidedly plays second fiddle to assimilation.

The relation between assimilation and accommodation changes dramatically in substages 4 and 5 when infants begin to take an active interest in the objects of actions. Through means-end coordination and systematic exploration, accommodation, corresponding to the specifics of various objects, becomes increasingly differentiated. Whereas before the interest was focused on the assimilating activity (e.g., grasping), now the interest shifts to the variously interesting things to which schemes can be accommodated. Two novelties are noted. One, as mentioned before, is that newness as such becomes a challenge and the occasion for an active compensatory response; the other, the accommodatory function (in itself the negative of the action-object) takes on a positive character in the shape of intentional signals and intentional imitation.

Earlier forms of imitation can be explained as the continuation of on-going actions. Now, however, children can imitate actions that are new or can only be seen in others, not on their own person. These imitations require an active modality transfer from visual to movement accommodation. Children observe a person who opens the mouth or sticks out the tongue. How can one explain the systematic imitation and differentiation of these two situations—barring of course any form of learning by trial and reinforcement? Piaget postulates that children know what opening-of-the-mouth and sticking-out-the-tongue "means," not merely in action (they have done this before) but in visual accommodation. This is what is meant by "positive," in that accommodation functions like a positive signal that allows children to transfer a visual model to their own invisible movement. But how would they differentiate these two situations? Here Piaget noticed the use of an intentional signal (he called it "index"), namely, the different sounds involuntarily produced in the two situations. Very soon after the children became aware of the difference in sounds, both in the model and in their own imitation, sound could be altogether eliminated and imitation was successful by vision alone. Piaget saw here in the use of the index the beginning of the representative function—representation that is still tied to action, but nevertheless a clear forerunner of fully symbolic representation as shown in the car playing of the three-year-old child.

Object knowledge—an action-differentiated knowledge—makes symbol formation possible. It should be clear why this is so because symbol can be defined as an action-differentiated signifier. Sensorimotor action-knowledge includes communication, learned signals, and even intersensory indices. But all these are undifferentiated signifiers. The signifier is part of the signified action. In symbols, however, the signifier is no longer tied to the action, but is a separate entity. The block of wood and its movement are in no way part of the car-action. If there is a connection between them, it is not a present-action-connection but a relation of mental implication: the moving block signifies the car-action (the signified). In Piaget's terminology, the accommodation to the car is separated from the perception of the present car and as a "positive" serves a representative function. Through this type of representative accommodation, the block becomes a symbol of the car.

In addition to a symbolic accommodation there is also a present action accommodation to the block; after all, the child is holding the block and moving it. But this present accommodation is decidedly secondary, so much so that any other thing that conveniently can be held would do. In fact, as will be shown in the following paragraph, the child could play car without any material substitute at all, simply moving the fist; and even this movement can be dispensed with. The symbolic *connection* of signifier-signified must be seen as the other side of the coin of the preceding object-action *disconnection*. Both the connecting and disconnecting are developmentally acquired knowledge achievements and are acts done by the subject. These are the acts that establish a knowing subject vis-à-vis the known object. Here then, if you like, is the beginning of thought as well as the first step on the way to objective knowledge.

One further step in symbol formation was just indicated and must have occurred to the readers for some time. Adults as a rule no longer engage in symbolic play. Apart from social traditions, customs, and especially the verbal language in its different social uses, our main symbols are internal in the form of mental images or internal narratives. The process of internalizing symbols does in fact begin at the same time as symbolic play is observed, and it is this internalization of symbols above all that is decisive for human psychology. Consider what it involves. Nothing more or less than the construction of a world, different from the preceding present-action world, a world no longer necessarily constrained by the resistances of other people or physical causality. Playing car by moving a block is not subject to the constraints of the real world of cars and traffic. But there are limits, if only those described by the reach of the arm and the presence of the furniture. Remove all these limits and you find yourself in a truly limitless world of internal symbols, subject to no other constraint than the desires of the assimilating "I."

Children who play car in imagination can drive the car through the air or under water or do anything else with the car according to their fancy. Piaget calls this playful relaxation from reality constraints a "distorting assimilation" since it is the assimilation of reality to personal desires, and he considers the socialization of the symbol as the major knowledge task for the period beginning with symbol formation. This socialization proceeds in a double direction, one toward the construction of a system of shared logical rules (Piaget's "operation"), the other toward the coordination of other people's viewpoints ("co-operation"). Symbolism expresses the child's present reality, writes Piaget:

> Since it derives from assimilation, one of the aspects of intelligence from the beginning, symbolism first expands this assimilation in an egocentric direction, and then, with the double progress of interiorization of the symbol towards representative construction, and expansion of thought towards conceptualization, symbolic assimilation is reintegrated in thought in the form of creative imagination. (1946:163).

"Interiorization" refers here to the logical operations of shared internal actions, while "conceptualization" refers to the conventional concepts involved in verbal interchange.

Note that Piaget does not hesitate to characterize the whole psychology of the child from about age two to age six as a playful "symbolism," and he connects it with the assimilatory function of knowledge. This is the principal reason why pretend play was chosen as the most typical form of the symbolic function. Because assimilation transforms reality according to available knowledge schemes, there is both a playful and a deforming quality in every assimilation unless this is counteracted by the assimilation being in balance with the imitative-submissive quality of accommodation.

The developmental origin of the symbolic object as signifier has been discussed and related to the accommodatory function. Now the source of symbolic playfulness is assigned to the assimilatory function. Long before the time of symbol formation, infants engage in playful assimilations, such as the early functional and generalizing sensorimotor assimilations when infants repeat and practice fortuitous action patterns for no other purpose than the pleasure of the action (practice play). At substage 4 there is even evidence of pretend actions in the shape of a pleasurable ritualization of an action which is purposeful in a different situation. An example would be a going-to-sleep action, occasioned by the presence of the pillow, when the infant has no intention of going to sleep. Why is this not symbolic play but only, as Piaget (1946:101, 112) suggests something halfway between practice play and symbolic play? For two reasons: first, the signifier (the pillow) is still part of the signified action (sleeping), second, the child has no awareness of pretending, that is, the object-disconnecting and the symbolic connecting is not yet fully established.

A few months later, the same child indicates awareness of pretense by shaking the head and saying "No-no." Now there is object and symbol construction with the child intentionally doing the pretending, even though the signifier is still an ordinary part of the action. A three-year-old boy who plays car has gone a step further in using as a symbol something that is quite separate from the car-action. He too has the intention of playing and is aware of pretending. (He may not care about the difference of play and reality, but this is another matter). With the internalization of the symbol as a mental image, the symbol is fully separated as an element of thought and takes on a life of its own.

This then is the birth of symbolic thought. The action-separated object-of-knowledge is psychologically present (i.e., re-presented) to the child. From the viewpoint of knowledge, symbolic presence is not something that is simply there, to be taken as a given and present at the birth of the child. A biological-developmental framework recognizes that such a capability cannot be innate or preformed as a neurological entity. Rather, it is a psychological achievement and requires for its explanation a psychological history. We have followed the history from birth to about age three as outlined in Piaget's research. The internal symbol is described as the outcome of the interplay of the twin processes, basic to every level of biological knowledge, assimilation and accommodation. Accommodation provides the child with the representational element necessary for symbolic thought, assimilation with playfulness in the use of these elements.

At this point I refer back to chapter 1, in which I characterized symbolic actions as requiring a motivation over and beyond the present action. The question I am asking concerns the psychological connection between symbols and playfulness: why are spontaneous symbols at first used in a playful manner? Piaget systematically examined the logical stages leading to the child's symbolism. His definition of play as the assimilation of reality to the child's desires points to the motivation behind play, but the motivation as such remained unexamined. In the rest of the essay I propose to defend the thesis that the child's desires have a meaningful connection—in the context of human evolution—with the child's symbolic function. Accordingly, I would answer the above question by saying that unless children first assimilated reality to their desires, they would never go to the trouble of constructing a symbolic world and—for good or evil—suffer its consequences.

3.

The Formation
of the Unconscious World

FREUD PUBLISHED HIS *Interpretation of Dreams* in 1900. It was, if
not his first psychoanalytic work, certainly the first in which he
engaged in extensive psychological theorizing ("metapsychol-
ogy") on the basis of his psychoanalytic experience alone and
discarded altogether any pretense of clothing his theoretical exposition in a neurological garb. The immediate occasion for this
work was the death of Freud's father three years earlier, which
brought about a period of intense emotional upheaval and Freud's
disciplined resolve to get to the bottom of it. In order to achieve
this self-imposed task, Freud started to interpret his own dreams;
this enterprise turned out to be the world's first psychoanalytic
treatment. Freud was forty-one years old at the time of his father's
death, and forty-four when the book was published. The publication, reporting dark conflicting areas in the depth of the human
soul, hardly caused a ripple in the complacent optimism of the
pre-World War European intelligentsia. Was not science about to
banish the last remnants of the dark forces of superstition and
magic? The road to inevitable all-around betterment seemed wide

open, and people were pushed in the right direction both by the material advances from outside and by a supposed instinct toward ever greater perfection from inside.

With the senseless slaughter of World War I, Western optimism finally collapsed. In the aftermath of that traumatic experience and the necessary mental reappraisal, Freud's ideas became relevant and rapidly spread throughout the Western world. In contrast to Freud, when Piaget (born 1896, forty years after Freud) was in his twenties, he had already published his first major works, which were enthusiastically received. Moreover, he had some personal contact with psychoanalysis. In addition to extensive reading Piaget even spent some time in a didactic analysis. He also delivered a paper at the 1922 psychoanalytic congress in Berlin with Freud in attendance. His aim was to demonstrate that the unconscious that psychoanalysis claimed to be the province of repression and neurosis is not alien to normal thinking, that assimilation was always something of an unconscious process. His views were welcomed, but no more. The aims of the by now established psychoanalytic science—to probe the deepest motivational sources of human conduct—and of Piaget's fledgling direction—to explore the developmental origins of logical thinking—were too far apart to allow any cross-fertilization. Nevertheless, Piaget remained basically sympathetic to Freud's ideas and in his *Symbol Formation*, published 1946, devoted a whole section to "unconscious" symbolism, in which he related his own theory of symbol formation to Freud's.

In a sense, then, I continue in this essay a dialogue that could have started some sixty years ago. I believe that at this early date with the best of intentions the two views, a philosophy of knowledge turned empirical science and a psychoanalysis of emotions, could not have gotten together. Psychological and historical reasons militated against it. It certainly could not be done by the founding persons whose original insights created the respective sciences. Like all genuine innovators, they needed the undivided focus of their own personal perspectives. With regard to the prevailing intellectual climate at that time, while it was favorable to recognizing the status of emotions, the personal and the existential, science and logical reason were still kept apart. Only the latter two were "objective," the others were relegated to the "subjective." After another world war and the awareness that our most advanced reason has created, but cannot solve, an existentially most destructive nuclear situation, only now is it perhaps possible to conceive of knowledge not as something apart from emotions, but to treat knowledge as a special form of emotion and vice versa. As a preliminary to this integrated view, I shall present what I consider Freud's chief psychological themes, starting with the formation of dreams as the key example of Freud's position on what we have learned in previous chapters to call symbol formation.

DREAM-FORMATION

First, it is important to realize that Freud used the word symbol in a greatly restricted sense. For him symbols are internal images that are only indirectly or figuratively related to what they signify and transcend the individual's personal experience. Freud discovered that these images were found in many people who were not aware of their symbolic nature. He was inclined to explain them as if they were an inherited psychological tendency. Such symbols would frequently relate to sexual fantasies and because of their generality could be interpreted without exploring personal associations. (Other dream images, Freud held, could be interpreted only by way of personal associations.) On this specific point, Freud's speculation seems to come closest to what is commonly accepted as Jung's "collective unconscious."

Yet in other places, Freud was quite opposed to Jung's position and to the all too facile reliance on inherited schemas instead of "following the correct procedure of observing instances and pushing the inquiry through the stages of individual acquisition" (1918 12:156). I believe this is a clear instance where Freud was not at all dogmatic and merely suggested a hypothetical innateness for lack of a ready developmental theory. Piaget, as we shall see, followed Freud's admonition to the letter and proposed an individual acquisition both of Freud's symbols and all of Jung's collective unconscious.

Within Piaget's theory a dream image, like any mental image, falls fully within the scope of a symbol. It is a form of "making psychologically present" something that perceptually is not present. As a symbol the dream image points to something beyond itself, namely, its meaning. To get to the meaning, Freud proposed a stepwise interpretation starting with what is superficially available to the dreamer who on being awake recounts a dream. This portion Freud called "the manifest dream." It is, however, not the dream itself, merely the product of the "dream work," and according to Freud this dream work is really the dream. So the dream is an unconscious activity that produces the manifest, "conscious" dream. The dream work is so named because it works on a particular content, namely, "the latent dream thought," which is again not the dream proper but the occasion for the dream. The latent thought is preconscious in itself and points in two directions: toward the conscious activity of the previous day and toward the unconscious activity of the sleeper's dream work. In its first direction, it is connected with what Freud called the day's residue, some conscious thought of sufficient affect so that it tries to occupy the sleeper's awareness despite the general lowering of attention to the outside world during sleep. The day's residue accomplishes this task, Freud held, by attaching itself to the latent thought, a connection that may even have been present during the day. What then is the peculiar quality of the latent thought that cannot be fulfilled by just any thought and makes this alliance between the day's thought and the latent dream thought necessary?

Here we come to Freud's most original but also most controversial and misunderstood insight. As said above, the latent thought is two-faced. It is, or can be, connected to conscious activity, and in this sense it is preconscious and the day's residue can use it for its purpose. But the latent thought is also open toward unconscious activity. Unconscious wishes and impulses can express themselves through it. It is like a small opening through which intimate affective drives and wishes, usually held at check, can rush out into the conscious mentality. This is at a time when, due to sleep, the usual vigilance vis-à-vis the unconscious is lowered. (Since dream activity stays on a symbolic, action-disconnected level, there is no physical or psychological danger to self or others.) In short, the unconscious wish provides the psychological energy, the motivation of dream formation, and the latent thought is welcome to the unconscious wish in so far as it lends itself to express the wish as fulfilled.

But this wish is something adults would never consciously admit, and the fulfillment of the wish is even less likely to be experienced as part of their conscious or preconscious psychology. Nevertheless, during sleep the wishful impulses are stronger and the usual conscious vigilance is weaker than when awake. A serious psychological disturbance in the form of anxiety would awaken the potential dreamer and frustrate the intent to sleep. The function of dream work is to avoid this anxiety. The latent thought activity is turned into a dream activity and the product of the dream is the manifest content. The dream can now be seen as a typical example of a compromise between two conflicting tendencies. On a superficial level, it both threatens—by introducing repressed material into conscious awareness—and maintains—by the dream production—the continuation of the sleep. On a deeper level the dream expresses the fulfillment of an unconscious wish; but at the same time it disguises the expression and connects it to the day's residue to make it acceptable to the conscious person (who is repressing the wish).

Dream work does not proceed according to the constraints of logic or reality or reasonable presentation. Instead, Freud recognized two general tendencies of the dream work, which he named displacement and condensation. Displacement refers to all kinds of transformations over time, place, events; most particularly the separation of the affect from the appropriate image and inversions, such as from the negative to the positive, from the active to the passive. Condensation is at work when a part of an image stands for the whole (synecdoche) or when one image has multiple meanings. Here, Freud believed, was evidence that unconscious psychology works in ways that are vastly different from the operations of the conscious, logical mind. He noted particularly that the unconscious knows neither negation nor delay of gratification: to express a wish means to express it as fulfilled.

The interpretation of dreams became for Freud the royal road to fathom the workings of the unconscious. It also became the model for the understanding of neurotic symptoms which, like dreams, involved compromises between conflicting tendencies within the person. Neuroticism is a difficult enough concept to specify in its various forms. Can it be differentiated from the normal humdrum of personal idiosyncratic existence in a particular culture with its own relative standards of normalcy? Beyond that, Freud and his associates extended the insights gained from dream formation to many other areas of ordinary life, including artistic production and social group formation. With the spread of Freudian ideas and the corresponding increase of psychological "honesty," the dividing line between neurotic and normal has become fuzzy indeed. Freud's discovery that similar psychological processes were at work in ordinary dreams and in neurotic symptoms contributed to the general acceptance that to be human means to have neurotic tendencies and that a person free of any neurotic process—even as an ideal—is an unreality.

While Freud's general insights have gained such widespread recognition that some of his technical terms have become part of ordinary language, his specific theoretical model of dream formation is by no means widely accepted or, for that matter, well understood. This is even the case with practicing psychoanalysts who use Freud's method of dream interpretation. They follow Freud's lead in that they are not at all interested in the manifest dream. Rather, by means of free association they focus on the latent thought and the conflicting unconscious forces around it. This is the therapeutically important component. They are then satisfied that in the latent thought they have reached behind the manifest to the "real" dream. But this is a conceptual misunderstanding.

On more than one occasion, Freud reminded his audience that the latent thought is not the dream but merely the psychological occasion, just as a peculiar body or sense impression could become the material occasion for dream formation:

> The day's residues are psychic material for the dream work, just as the accidentally present sense and body stimulations or experimentally induced conditions are its somatic material. To impart to them the chief role in dream formation would be nothing else than to repeat the pre-analytic error at a new location. Latent dream thoughts are not assigned to the dream but to the preconscious thinking. The dream's quality of being a wish fulfillment must not be placed at one level with its quality of being a warning, a confession, an attempt at solving a problem, etc. (1913 10:18–19)

What Freud is saying may not make much difference in therapeutic practice, but it is decisive for his theoretical model. It is not the case that a person first has a "latent dream" and then by means of the dream work translates it into the "manifest dream." Freud wanted to be sure that the latent thought be related to its active affective, not its passive image component.

This affective component has the psychological reality of a wish in contrast to the dream, which is experienced as something known or perceived, hence Freud's reference in the above quote to the dream and the latent thought as not belonging to the same level of psychological reality. Freud is partly to blame for this frequent confusion. By naming this dream component "latent thought," indeed "latent dream thought," he led philosophically less sophisticated readers to make that very error he wanted to avoid.

> Latent dream thoughts are similar to usual conscious psychological products. They can be described as preconscious and in fact could have been conscious for a moment during the day. But by being joined to unconscious impulses during the night, they are assimilated to these impulses and, as it were, are pulled down to the state of unconscious thoughts and subject to the laws regulating unconscious activity. (1912 8:438)

Note here almost the same language that Piaget would later use: latent thoughts are assimilated to the child's activity and impulses. Is this a case where Freud, lacking a viable developmental theory of the formation of symbolic images and consciousness, "knew" more than he could clearly articulate? I think so. Nevertheless it is a mark of genius that the core of his thinking relative to the dynamics of dream formation can be integrated with the full-blown developmental theory of Piaget, constructed some fifty years later from entirely different premises. At the same time, it provides the key affective element missing from Piaget's theory with which to turn an epistemological into a fully integrated psychological theory of knowledge development.

I summarize Freud's dynamic theory of dreams as clearly as possible. To explain an adult's dream, Freud postulated six simultaneously interacting personal activities: (a) a conscious wish to sleep; (b) an unconscious infantile wish pressing for fulfillment; (c) the preconscious residue of the day's conscious activity; (d) a present preconscious impression of the state of the body and senses; (e) the habitual, though during sleep somewhat lowered pressure to keep the unconscious wish from becoming conscious; (f) the unconscious dream work producing the dream as a compromise in response to the conflicting pressures of the wish to sleep, the unconscious wish, and the habitual repression of the unconscious wish. The affect of the unconscious wish provides the psychological energy and the basic motivation (the "why?") of the dream. This wish needs the occasion of the day's preconscious residue or present sense impressions to enter (in a disguised form) the preconscious activity of the person. It has to overcome the resistance of repression, just as the two preconscious or conscious components, the day's residue and the impression of the state of the body, need the energy of the unconscious wish to overcome the wish to sleep. The dream work that disguises the infantile wish and, properly speaking, produces the preconscious ("manifest") dream, proceeds on the same psychological level of unconscious activity as the basic wish itself. In short, for Freud a dream is the product of an unconscious activity that works against a habitual repression to re-present a wish derivative as fulfilled;

the wish itself is part of the person's unconscious mentality and provides the affective energy for dream formation: "Dream is a (disguised) fulfillment of a (repressed) wish" (1924b 13:415).

Two more observations are crucial in this discussion of Freud's theory of dream formation. In childhood when the separation of unconscious from preconscious activity is not yet well established, the dream wish does not necessarily encounter the opposing force of repression and can then be represented as fulfilled without any elaborate disguise. The second observation also relates to childhood. Freud postulated that the dream work of adults is literally a developmental regression in which the relaxation during sleep permits adults to act according to a psychology typical of early childhood but abandoned later on. He called it primary process psychology and succinctly described the difference between unconscious and conscious activity as the difference between primary and secondary thought processes. For the time being, we can identify primary processes as "childlike" and secondary as "adult" thinking, while waiting for a more elaborate developmental elaboration of these terms. However, the concepts of the unconscious, preconscious, and repression have been frequently used, and we turn to a discussion of these Freudian themes.

THE UNCONSCIOUS

If Freud is known for anything, it is his exploration of the "unconscious" in human psychology. It must be remembered that he wrote at a time when the founders of what turned out to become the empirical science of psychology attempted to ground the new field in a systematic observation of the "soul," the main attribute of which was its being "conscious." In contrast, Freud followed a dynamic principle of searching for the causes of certain conducts. In pursuing this goal, he discovered what he called "the effective unconscious"—hidden psychological forces responsible for certain observable psychological effects that were not available to the consciousness of the individuals concerned. More than that, most people would at first vehemently deny that they harbored any such thoughts or wishes that analysts ascribed to their "unconscious." From the start of psychoanalysis, the contrast of conscious versus unconscious was not merely a descriptive qualification but represented a clash of opposing forces within a person: resistance, repression, negative investment, and censor are some of the concepts that signify the potential conflict between opposing tendencies.

To take care of the fact that there are innumerable things of which we are not consciously aware but, if need be or the occasion arises, of which we could become conscious, Freud used the adjective *preconscious*. What is preconscious and what is unconscious are not present to consciousness. However, what is preconscious could be made conscious, whereas this is not the case with unconscious material. Even though the terminology is quite crude and the underlying theory of consciousness is tied to a static theory of perception and truth (the German word for perception is *Wahrnehmung*, and it implies that conscious perception is the criterion of truth), it serves its purpose as long as we use preconscious as a subdivision of conscious and permit all kinds of gradations along several "dimensions" of consciousness, such as awareness, attention, understanding. Psychologically, Freud's preconscious is part of the conscious; between them there may be quantitative but not qualitative differences.

Freud's unconscious, however, is qualitatively different from the conscious, and this is what Freud expressed when he referred to separate psychological regions or separate parts of the personality. He stressed their separateness and the psychological barrier that keeps them apart. The more common description is the unconscious pressing against the conscious while the conscious is pressing back to keep the unconscious in place. Sometimes, as will be shown, the opposite picture is presented: the unconscious protecting itself against the invasion of conscious forces. Throughout, Freud used a highly plastic and substantive vocabulary, as if these were separate regions of the psyche with their own little persons controlling them. But this should not be a serious obstacle for someone who wants to comprehend the complexity and the contrariness, if not contradictoriness, of the psychological forces working within a person. More serious is the objection that Freud's theory of the unconscious could be used in evading personal responsibility. On this issue I only want to make one pertinent remark. Both Freud and Piaget were great iconoclasts and "relativizers." They rejected absolutes whether in terms of truth and knowledge or of personal freedom and responsibility and they avoided the extremes, either of affirmation or of negation, as equally untrue, unscientific, and potentially harmful. In fact I will attempt to show in this essay that their theories together can provide an adequate picture which links objective knowledge and personal responsibility—tracing their developmental history, their characteristic functions, possibilities and limits.

Initially Freud believed he could assign different drives to the two personality parts: the sexual drives to the unconscious, the ego drives to the conscious. Insofar as these drives have different objectives, the conflicts surrounding the psychological regions could be explained as a consequence of the different drives. A further simplification would be to align primary processes with the unconscious, secondary processes with the conscious. Eventually, this division proved to be too rigid and artificial. In this first scheme, there was only one possible answer to the question, what are the forces that keep the unconscious in check? They cannot be anything but forces emanating from the conscious, the region of the ego drives. But Freud observed frequently that the ego and superego forces pressing down on the unconscious were themselves as unconscious (strictly speaking) as the unconscious itself. A revision was in order, and it was introduced in 1920, at the same time as Freud revised the model of the two opposing drives.

Instead of different psychological regions, Freud now referred to three different agencies: the *id,* the *ego,* the *superego.* Everything that is in the id is unconscious, but the activities of both the ego and particularly the superego are also unconscious to a great part; more precisely, only a small part of the ego and perhaps an even smaller part of the superego are conscious or preconscious. Now Freud no longer considered the sexual and the ego drives as opposed; they became included in the eros drive, and its opposition was the destruction drive. The great winner, if I can say so, in this new model was the ego. It is no longer seen as closed up against the unconscious. On the contrary, it is pictured in fluid continuity with the id, considered as the great reservoir of the drives, so that the ego can take into itself some of these unconscious forces. Similarly, the conscious part is no longer equipped with its own ego drive opposing the unconscious part with its own sexual drive; rather the two new drives, eros and destruction, are said to permeate all personality parts, another indication of the openness of the ego toward the id and vice versa.

It is understandable that Freud in his early writings focused on the unconscious as that part of a person that had been neglected by contemporary philosophical, academic, and medical psychology. He treated consciousness and the conscious "I" as something given and taken for granted. If he had any theory about consciousness at all, it was related, as indicated earlier, to the conscious verbalized awareness of a perception. The unconscious was then described as something that was not or could not be "lit up" by the daylight of perception.

As Freud paid increasing attention to the "I", or as it is commonly translated, the ego, he realized that it did not make sense to ascribe to the new-born infant anything like an ego: "A unity analogous to the ego is not present to the individual at birth; the ego must be developed" (1914 10:142). When he introduced his new personality model Freud maintained this developmental perspective and insisted that the id-ego separation must not be taken too rigidly. Along with this developmental insight came Freud's conviction that a radical separation of ego drives and sex drives was not adequate to psychological reality. The concept of narcissism was his way of getting the two drives together, not long before he abandoned their separation completely and included them in the one eros drive. In fact, the above quote on the ego is taken from his essay on narcissism and the following sentence states plainly that "the auto-erotic drives are there from the beginning."

A more detailed discussion of a number of points must be left for later as we concentrate in this section on the unconscious, Freud's special object of study. We ask, following up the last sentence, is there an unconscious from the beginning? I believe Freud would have answered with a yes, because in his thinking about the unconscious he did not differentiate between the drive component and the knowledge component. In fact, he concentrated his concern almost exclusively on the affect component as was pointed out above in connection with the latent dream thought. "This disavowed thought, or better, this particular impulse," is one clear instance where Freud (1933 15:28) corrected himself, indicating that in the psychology of dream formation what matters is not so much the thought in the form of knowledge as the impulse to which the thought (image, fantasy) is assimilated. And this impulse, Freud continued, derives from the unconscious.

Now if the unconscious refers primarily to drives and impulses and only secondarily to knowledge content, then there is no difficulty in postulating its presence at birth. "Consciousness in the child is not easy to differentiate from the unconscious . . . it is incomplete, still in development and cannot readily be verbally expressed" (1918 12:139). When Freud refers here to the conscious-unconscious contrast and subsequently links the conscious with what can be verbally expressed, should we say the child first has unconscious knowledge and from that beginning slowly develops conscious knowledge? That does not seem to make sense.

Another more plausible interpretation would be the proposition that infants start with preconscious *drives* and in the course of development attain a conscious ego with reasonable knowledge and emotions. But this statement is woefully inadequate if the basic premise of Freud is left out of consideration. This premise is the continuous presence of the unconscious in adults. With this in mind, read what Freud says about the unconscious a few pages later.

Considering the evidence of dreams and neuroses in early childhood, Freud expressed his conviction that "a kind of knowledge, difficult to define, something like a preparatory stage of understanding, is effective in the child" (1918 12:156). He could not imagine the nature of this knowledge, "the only basis for a possible answer could be found in the interesting analogy with the extensive instinctual knowledge of animals." On the previous page Freud speculated on

> phylogenetically acquired schemata which like the philosophical "categories" enable the appropriation of experiences. I am of the opinion that they are imprints of human cultural history. The Oedipus complex, concerned with the relations of the child to the parents, belongs there, and is in fact the best known instance of its kind. Where experiences do not fit the hereditary schema, they will be worked over in fantasy. . . . The clash of experience versus schema seems to provide plenty of material for infantile conflicts. (1918 12:155)

From this citation I would like to single out two ideas for later discussion: Freud's reference to Kant's schemata and *a priori* categories of understanding and his comments on instinctual tendencies based on the evolutionary history of mankind. While the first is a major philosophical issue to be explored in chapter 6 in connection with Piaget's theory, the second is a biological issue and will be a major focus of the next two chapters. In the meantime, note Freud's developmental perspective concerning preforms of knowledge present in young children—in the case Freud is discussing, the youngest age to which he refers is one and a half years. Let this be said in case someone is tempted to interpret Freud's word "instinctual" with "present at birth." He continued:

> If there would be such an instinctual possession in humans, it would not be surprising if it were concerned with the processes of psychosexuality without necessarily being limited to these. This instinctual [factor] would be the nucleus of the unconscious, a primitive mental activity. Even though later on dethroned and overlaid by the developing reason, it would frequently, perhaps with all people, retain the power to pull higher psychological processes down to its level. Repression would be the return to this instinctual stage and humans would pay for their new achievement by their potential for neuroses. The significance of early childhood traumas would be to furnish the unconscious with material which protects it from being consumed by subsequent development. (1918 12:156)

Freud's use of the word *instinctual* needs a comment, specifically since his word for "drive" (German, *Trieb*) as mentioned earlier, is invariably and confusingly translated as "instinct." But note that he connects *instinct* with knowledge (as indeed it should be done), not with drives, and he calls it a primitive mental activity, a pre-stage of knowing and understanding, preparatory to the development of mature logical reason. He pictures children constructing "phylogenetically derived schemata," that is, a general knowledge framework, to which they incorporate (or in Piaget's terms: "assimilate") their individual significant experiences. He assumes that children experience interpersonal relations in the form of bodily (Freud says "sexual") impulses toward their caretakers whom they now fantasize as objects of attachment. This early attempt at giving meaning to their experiences is surrounded by conflicts of the severest type. Freud speaks here of traumas and childhood neuroses. This in itself was a startling observation that developmental psychologists, anxious to confirm the popular picture of a happy, conflict-free childhood, were slow to accept.

But even more remarkable is Freud's conclusion that repression and trauma, even (or particularly) at this early age, are indispensable and have a functional significance. They become the occasion for consolidating unconscious activity and providing it with personally meaningful content. So equipped, the unconscious can repel the onslaught of conscious reason, most conspicuously at the time of the dissolution of the Oedipus complex, and it can periodically lure conscious material down to its level in the nightly compromise of dream formation or the psychologically more severe and lasting compromise of symptom and character formation.

In discussing the nature of Freud's unconscious, I started by stressing the drive component in terms of affect or emotions. I was prepared to accept that drives were present from the beginning of human life. But with the reference to instinctual schemata, an organizing knowledge element is introduced somewhere between the ages of one and two, leading to the formation of such psychological products as fantasy, dreams, and unconscious material. These are symbolic products that Freud studied in terms of *why*, i.e., their individual history—and Piaget later on explored in terms of *how*, i.e., their logical organization. The schemata of understanding and the mental activities mentioned by Freud are indeed Piaget's knowledge schemes of the permanent object and of action-separated symbols as discussed in the preceding chapter. This point in development, I suggest, is the birth of the unconscious considered as a psychological region filled with drive impulses and unconscious fantasies.

Perhaps the discussion will gain in clarity if instead of the unconscious and the conscious as a region, we now adopt Freud's own modification from the regional (topographical) to the action (dynamic) model—he himself called the id and the ego "agencies" in the sense of source of actions. The action model suggests the active doing of a person in contrast to a static psychological region where the unconscious is pictured as residing. This switch in perspective is similar to Freud's identification of the dream with its underlying dream work rather than its manifest or latent dream image. The word *unconscious* can then be limited to its much more sensible adjectival use as an action which in its results is unconscious.

Another comment is in order relative to the adjective "unconscious" and requires a brief digression into the notion of consciousness. The word *unconscious* should really be read as hyphenated with the *un-* implying an active doing of something, an undoing, if you like, a repelling or a repressing. In short—and contrary to Freud's speculation, even though in accord with his stress on the dynamics of unconscious material—I hold that whatever in a person is now unconscious was at some earlier time *made* to be unconscious. Unfortunately Freud had an inadequate picture of consciousness. He thought of it as the light of a lamp by which a person can observe an internal perception and report it verbally. This is in any case a special type of being conscious, which as a minimum requires object formation and some degree of concept formation. To accomplish this consciousness, I must stand as an "I" against something that I observe as an object (of knowledge) of some kind.

We have previously discussed the useful concept of "preconscious." For many reasons it should be included in the more general concept of "conscious" and clearly separated from "unconscious." It is not easy to draw the exact line between the conscious and preconscious. Are you conscious of what you are doing when you walk to the door? Certainly, but only to a degree. A vast, an indefinite amount of possible perceptual material is only preconscious. A ten-month-old baby girl making her first steps is conscious of (that is, is paying attention to) all kinds of spatial configurations and bodily positions. Much of this will very soon become habitual and preconscious.

In Piaget's theory consciousness is generally linked to the object of an action, more precisely the accommodation component of an action responding to the "resistance" of the object; whereas the assimilation component, including the internal scheme (of assimilation), is not conscious, unless on special occasions it becomes an object of self-reflection. I believe that it was something like this that Piaget wanted to tell the Freudians assembled in Berlin, but he used the word "unconscious" where above I put "not conscious" or "preconscious." Piaget would often say "assimilation is an unconscious process," whereas it would be better to say "it is not a conscious process," particularly when speaking in a context where "unconscious" has a special dynamic meaning.

Freud pictured the id part of the personality as the primary agency that deals with the interplay of the basic drives. In the adult the id activity is entirely unconscious in the strong Freudian sense. This is in contrast to the ego's activity, which at least in part is conscious. The id agency works according to the pleasure principle and primary mental processes; in the ego—at least in part—the reality principle and secondary mental processes are the corresponding qualities. For Freud the great dividing event that definitely separates the ego (and its characteristic actions) from the id is the resolution of the Oedipus complex, around age six. This involves the final giving up of a first, self-centered mental life, constructed over the first five years by the young child, and a resolute turning toward the wider world of social reality. Freud refers to this great divide in no uncertain terms as a veritable emotional upheaval. It is a "destruction" surrounded by most painful and humiliating personal experiences. It is a repression, in fact, it is the primal repression in relation to which all later repressions are mere secondary symptoms, a follow-up *(Nachdrängen)* to the original repression *(Urverdrängung)*.

PRIMAL REPRESSION

          I list this as a special Freudian theme because the concept of repression is widely known in its secondary adult form, whereas from a developmental viewpoint primal repression is the really crucial event that marks the psychology of every human being. Freud was aware that his theory was strong on follow-up repression but weak on primal repression:

> Repressions encountered in therapy are mostly instances of follow-up repression. They presuppose earlier primal repressions that exert their attraction upon the later situations. Much too little is known about these origins and pre-forms of repression. Consider the role of the superego in repression, which can be easily overrated. It is not yet possible to decide whether perhaps the formation of the superego is the transition from primal to follow-up repression. In any case the first and very intensive attacks of anxiety are experienced at a time prior to the differentiation of the superego. It is quite plausible that the immediate occasions of primal repressions are quantitative moments such as an excessive force of excitation and a breach of the protective mechanism. (1926 14:121)

          To clarify the origins of primal repression, it would help to treat it as an integral component of the first symbolic world that children construct. But this first construction and repression should not be taken as something that takes place once for all at one particular time. Rather, the Oedipus complex or fantasy can be accepted as Freud's name for an ongoing psychological activity in children for about four to five years, roughly age two to age six.

In it they attempt to make sense of themselves as persons in relation to the proximate world in which they live. This is a slow, gradual and expanding process of symbol formation that eventually becomes stabilized in internal images or fantasies.

The center of this mental world is the "I" or more precisely the "I want," that is, infantile wishes of intensive affective qualities. Actually the phrase "I want" is still inadequate; it should at the least be completed by the object of the want, which at that time is not just a vague feeling for something, but a very definite object the child desires and knows as such. Object formation is the psychological device that enables children around age two to know another person as a desirable object. This object is of course a quite concrete and bodily related other. "I want my object" would be a better paraphrase, but even this could impart the developmentally wrong impression, as if there is first an "I" that then comes to know and want the object. If I may put forward a chronological sequence, I would suggest that the wish comes first, the object second, and the "I" comes last. Stretching the point both temporally and conceptually, I could defend the notion that the wish is present from birth, the object appears at age two, and the "I" at age six.

The "want-object" is the substance of the oedipal world, a continuation of the preceding sensorimotor world where present objects were coordinated to present needs. But this continuation has a new element, namely, the knowledge of the permanent object. Now the "want-object" can be satisfied by means of symbol formation in which an absent object is made psychologically present.

The connection between want-object and symbol has far-reaching psychological consequences. If you consider the preceding sensorimotor development as a steady progression toward a surprisingly adequate understanding of present action constraints, symbol formation as action-separated knowledge with one stroke does away with these constraints. Now the wish for the object reigns supreme, unchecked by any constraints of physical or social reality or any laws of logical implication. This is true at least in those areas where the children cannot or do not share

their symbolic products with others. At this point primal repression becomes a functionally relevant mechanism to separate what
eventually will be established as the unconscious id in opposition
to the conscious ego.

Primal repression "presupposes a negative investment
through which the preconscious system protects itself from the
pressure of unconscious symbols" (1915c 10:280). Remember,
this takes place at a period in children's lives when the ego and
the id are not yet clearly separated, nor is the separation of unconscious and conscious activity well established. So what shall
we say to the legitimate question: who is doing the repressing and
who is doing the construction of the fantasies that are being
repressed? The answer is obvious: the children are doing it. This
is not something that simply happens to the children the way the
first teeth grow and subsequently fall out when the second push
up. In fact, Freud considered this view and admitted that there
was something of the nature of an instinct about the rise and
collapse of the Oedipus fantasy, somewhat as "at birth the individual as a whole is predetermined to die and perhaps the organic
disposition already contains a hint about the cause." Yet Freud
continued, "nevertheless it is of interest to investigate how the
innate program is executed, in what way contingent harmful
conditions exploit the organic disposition" (1924a 13:396).

Any truly developmental viewpoint constantly comes
across apparent paradoxes similar to the above maturation-de-
velopment issue. Take the problem of universality versus individual differences. Is a universal development by itself evidence that
there is no individual psychological development? Of course not!
We can firmly hold that the developmental theories of Piaget or
of Freud describe a general (if you like, universal) progression of
logical or psychosexual maturity without having to deny either
an innate directional disposition or the autonomy of the individual
agent. Both theories are badly misunderstood if one extreme is
emphasized at the expense of the other extreme.

To return to the question of the source of primal repression, the developmental perspective has to be kept firmly in mind
in order to avoid serious conceptual confusions. On the one hand,
for Freud repression is the mechanism that at any one time separates unconscious from conscious activity; on the other hand, it

is also the primary mechanism that during development brings about the establishment of these two mental qualities: "repression and unconscious are to a large extent correlative" (1915b 10:250). One can easily understand that conscious ego forces—directly or indirectly—repress forces emanating from the unconscious id. But primal repression is prior to the conscious-unconscious or the ego-id differentiation.

The developmental paradox is clear. How can there be anything to repress when there is not yet unconscious content, and how can the child do the repressing if there is not yet a conscious agent? The questions presuppose distinctions that are not yet developmentally fixed. As in the cases mentioned earlier, the paradox disappears with a clear conception of what psychological development implies.

Primal repression, like all repression, "is not some past event that happened once and is completed . . . rather repression requires an ongoing expenditure of energy" (1915b 10:253). In this manner think of primal repression as a process contemporaneous with the first symbolic world constructed by the children, a first phase of repression, as Freud calls it:

> There is reason to assume a primal repression, a first phase of repression; it consists in excluding a psychic (symbol-) representation from acceptance into consciousness. This amounts to a fixation; from now on the particular representation remains without change, with the drive bound to it. The second phase of repression, repression proper, concerns psychic derivatives of the repressed representation . . . repression proper is therefore a follow-up repression. Moreover it is inappropriate to emphasize exclusively the repulsive force from the conscious onto the material to-be-repressed. To the same extent there is the attraction exercised by the primal repressed material on everything with which it can establish some connections. The repressive tendency would probably not accomplish its goal if these two forces did not collaborate, if there were not some previously repressed material ready to accept what is rejected from the conscious. . . . Repression does not hinder the drive representation to continue in the unconscious, to organize further, to form derivatives and establish connections. . . . The drive representation develops more profusely and with less interference if through repression it is cut off from conscious influence. (1915b 10:250–251)

Here Freud introduced a second force operating in repression, an attraction that the unconscious exerts upon the conscious in addition to the force that repels or excludes from the conscious. Again, as in an earlier quote, the unusual picture of the unconscious as actively protecting itself from the conscious is invoked. The unconscious "fixates" a particular symbol-drive connection that then can proliferate and organize into an unconscious symbol life of its own, undisturbed by conscious influences.

These unconscious symbols, the result of primal repression, exercise a continuous attraction on the conscious activities. The psychological pull of this attraction is not merely the prime occasion of nightly dreams or of repression proper with its ensuing neurotic symptoms. It is the basis also of whatever is considered the best and highest in human endeavors and values. Neither Freud nor Piaget accepted the notion of a necessary progress in the form of a drive toward perfection. But then they had no need to postulate a special motor of progression. Tension and disequilibrium were built into their respective models of symbol and knowledge formation, along with the socially based capacity for newness and reconstruction. For Freud the eros drive together with the results of primal repression sufficed to explain personal development and any apparent or real social progress:

The repressed drive never gives up its desire for full satisfaction through repetition of a primal satisfying experience; all substitute-reaction-formations and sublimations are insufficient to eliminate the drive's continuing tension. The difference between the desired and the actual satisfaction results in the driving force which does not permit resting in any one situation . . . The way back to full satisfaction is, as a rule, blocked through the resistances that keep the repression going. Thus nothing else can be done than to proceed in the other developmental direction albeit with no expectation of completing the process and reaching the goal. (1920 13:44)

There can be no doubt that Freud refers here to repression in its primal form rather than to a secondary repression that is linked to particular neurotic symptoms. It is unfortunate although understandable that the secondary form with its connotation of psychological maladjustment was studied first and caught the attention of the public. As a consequence, primal repression, if it is recognized at all, is seen as the occasion of secondary repression (which it is), but its overall developmental role is not adequately appreciated. A child cannot become an adult without the personal action of primal repression; similarly, a culture free of all repression (*pace* H. Marcuse) is not even a good figment of the imagination.

In my view primal repression is the obligatory counterpart to what can be called primal symbol formation, the child's first construction of a symbolic world. Neither the construction nor the repression is something that is imposed on a passive child. On the contrary, in these two activities the children act and in acting become who they are. In the following quote, Freud's reference to the "first flowering of infantile sexuality" touches on what I called symbol formation, while its collapse is undoubtedly the most conspicuous example of primal repression.

> The first flowering of infantile sexuality was destined to come to naught due to the incompatibility of their wishes and reality as well as the inadequacy of the childish stage of development. It collapsed under most painful circumstances and experiences of deep hurt. The loss of love and the experience of failure left a permanent diminution of self worth. (1920 13:19)

Note the two conditions contributing to the downfall of the oedipal fantasy: first there is the resistance of reality, that is, insofar as the interpersonal reality is primary, the clash of personal wills, and second, the necessary experience of unequal power on the part of the child vis-à-vis the adult. By inadequacy Freud probably thought of lack of sexual development that precluded a mature love relation; but it does not falsify the sense if we include inadequacy of logical development. Indeed, once a first logical closure is achieved, it will give the child some measure of control over the private symbolic world and open up the vast possibilities of socialized reality.

Finally, in a developmental perspective, primal repression can be called the "cause" both of the unconscious and even of the conscious, insofar as these are two forms of adult psychology. If repression is the active, ongoing force that separates these two forms, it does not make sense to assign to one or the other priority in doing the first repressing. All we can say is that the same young children who are constructing an object- and a symbol-world, are also and at the same time constructing what eventually will become the conscious and the unconscious forms of this psychological world. But since this separation implies a mutual exclusion and a radically different way of dealing with drives, there must be a parting of ways early along the developmental path. I do not think that primal repression temporally coincides with what is commonly referred to as the collapse of the Oedipus fantasy, even though indeed it may be its final achievement. In any case around age six to seven the children have developed the divisions of the person as envisaged by psychoanalysis: there is an ego and a superego and an id; there is conscious (including preconscious) and unconscious knowledge; there is the psychology of primary and of secondary processes, of the pleasure and the reality principle.

In repression proper (as in dreams) there is the pull from the repressed material active in the id, together with the push away from the conscious (or preconscious) ego. This pushing away is pictured as a withdrawal of energy and is called a negative investment in contrast to the positive investment of the id activity. Freud speculated that primal repression is due to the negative investment alone, since there is nothing repressed as yet that could exercise a positive investment (as "the return of the repressed"). This insistence on a unilateral investment would not be necessary—it seems even somewhat against Freud's own dynamic theory of unconscious energy—provided we can take the radical developmental position of making the children's first symbolic constructions contemporaneous with the children's formation of a conscious, social ego and the formation of an unconscious, idiosyncratic id. With this formulation the previous answer as to who is doing the repressing becomes more meaningful. It is neither the ego nor the id—they are not yet definitely separated—but the children themselves as acting persons. Even as in development they safeguard their own individual psychology through primal repression, they move by the formation of logical operations toward a relative measure of personal freedom and social responsibility.

4.

Libido Bound
Through Symbols

FREUD REFERRED TO his drive theory as "our myth," something psychoanalytic psychology could not do without. He first adopted the two needs of love and hunger as the basis for distinguishing the sexual from the self-preservation drive, assigning to the first the interest in the other and to the second the interest in self. However, as his thought matured and as narcissism was incorporated as a sexual drive formation that had the self as its object, it became unsatisfactory to maintain the drive distinction. Similarly it proved impossible to limit consciousness to the self-preservation drives and unconsciousness to the sexual drives. For the last twenty years of his life, Freud held to the so-called second drive theory that postulated the contrast between life and death. The life drive, also called *eros*, was now identified with the former sexual drive together with its sexual energy or libido. But its extension was widened to include the whole spectrum of life, including also whatever was formerly attributed to the self-preservation drive.

This meant that, if Freud wished to keep a polarity in drives, he could no longer base it on content, rather he had to focus on the general quality or direction of the drives. For Freud the life drive functions according to the pleasure principle, and even the reality principle is now considered nothing else than a modification and socialization of the pleasure principle. In this connection the meaning of pleasure is moved even further away, as Freud had done from the beginning, from the mere selfish satisfaction of a biological need. It is the pleasure in making ever wider connections and constructing greater unities. I do not think that I misinterpret Freud's intention when within the framework of human development I equate Freud's eros with openness of the self toward the other and toward newness.

It follows that the opposing death drive can be conceptualized as a tendency toward closure or, better, closedness from the other or from any newness. It implies the direction of protecting the self (in opposition to interest in the other) and repeating familiar and routine life patterns (in opposition to constructing newness). Where this tendency becomes dominant, there is destruction, notably self-destruction and ultimately death. Freud based his speculations relative to the nature of the two drives on rather vague biological principles in addition to invoking the voice of myth and literature. To many, indeed, most of his associates and followers, Freud's arguments were not fully persuasive. It is therefore all the more interesting that Freud who was not at all aversive to changing his theoretical ideas, stayed with these two drives and even modified other theoretical concepts accordingly. Was it merely to oppose Jung, or if not that one personal reason, was it the only way to bring conflict into the inner core of human psychology? And does this not show that Freud was an inveterate pessimist as indeed many people claim him to be? I do not think so at all. But my aim here is not to produce a scholarly review of Freud's theoretical ideas, rather to note his most mature version of the two drives and see whether Piaget, another developmental psychologist, can provide more clarification and less mystification on this matter.

THE TWO BASIC DRIVES
UNDERLYING KNOWLEDGE AND EMOTIONS

Piaget's most crucial concept of his theory of knowledge is assimilation. It is a biological notion, almost equivalent to life itself. To respond to a particular situation by assimilation characterizes the action as alive since assimilation presupposes the existence of a living unit with its obligatory instruments of assimilation. As discussed in chapter 2, Piaget referred to an organism's schemes or schematism. In this biological perspective, every living action has an aspect of spontaneity relative to the underlying schemes and is therefore always more than a passive reaction to the external constraints of the situation. That these constraints exist goes without saying. That they determine in part the action or that without the constraints of the situation there could be no action is also clear. An action has to be done in a particular concrete situation and has to take account of its particulars. All this is taken care of by the concept of accommodation which is the concrete application of a scheme (of assimilation) to the constraints of the present situation. But accommodation alone is not a living response, but a mechanical reaction. It is the difference between a person accidentally plunging down from a height and a swimmer diving from the same height into the water. In both cases there is accommodation to gravity, but only in the second case is there a simultaneous assimilation of the gravity situation to the sensorimotor schemes of diving. Piaget insisted on assimilation, not in order to belittle the role of accommodation, but because too many scholars had exclusively focused on accommodation as the source of learning and knowledge, quite oblivious to the fact that it is schemes of assimilation that a person accommodates to objects of action or thinking.

The neglect of assimilation is perhaps not so serious when it is a question of routine action or habitual knowledge where schemes of the corresponding capacity are tacitly assumed. It is as a rule an easy matter of observation to explain a particular accommodation, such as walking around an obstacle (where the sensorimotor know-how of walking is assumed) or adding a particular sum (where operatory knowledge of numbers is assumed). These actions are in response to a given situation to reach or satisfy a certain goal. But when we deal with the construction of newness in knowledge, such as a new action know-how (e.g., using the rear window of a car), a new theoretical understanding (e.g., of numbers), a new social insight (e.g., the function of a retail store), it makes all the difference in the world whether we focus exclusively on the accommodation component or emphasize primarily the assimilation component. For now we are talking no longer about one concrete action but about a general understanding. What is the source of this new understanding and what is the motivation behind it? For accommodation there is, as just said, no problem: the external occasion and reward are usually quite apparent. But assimilation and schemes of assimilation are not observable as such nor are we directly aware of them as objects of introspection. All this is true and the possibility of uncontrolled theorizing in matters not directly observable must never be discounted. But going to the extreme of empiricism (which historically was a wholesome reaction to unbridled dogmatism) and identifying knowledge with the accommodation to given facts (the ideal of positivism) is, I feel, not only bad philosophy (but by whose criteria?), but an inadequate psychology and, above all, a radically deficient biology. A biology without assimilation is like music without sound.

Rather than throwing out the baby with the bath water, Piaget in his quest for a biologically valid theory of knowledge started with assimilation and schemes of assimilation and described how infants construct an ever more encompassing schematism of sensorimotor actions. Without saying it explicitly, Piaget takes for granted that children have a basic drive to assimilate. This by itself does not convey much until the meaning of assimilation is fully grasped. For the time being, we can accept that children have a general drive to use their schemes, and of course the only way to do this is to accommodate them to given situations.

Then why could one not say there is a basic drive to accommodate? Subsequent considerations will explain this more fully; however, consider that accommodation by itself is the *negative* imprint on the action from a resisting force, while assimilation is the *positive* imprint of the acting organism on a given situation. Accommodation is at the mercy of the fleeting moments and fortuitous contingencies, assimilation at all times implies at least some measure of autonomous control, if only in the limited sense that the organism is actively doing something.

But there is more to assimilation than the coordinating of outside material. The schemes themselves, as the source of assimilation, develop further and continue to make new connections and interconnections. It is Piaget's contention that the development of schemes is not to be seen as an added bonus due to favorable circumstances, but is intrinsic to the assimilation process. As said before, Piaget's is primarily a theory of development, and schemes of knowledge are precisely what develops. In Piaget's terse language, "the logic of development is the development of logic."

The most dramatic progress from biological reflex to the formation of the action-separated (permanent) object and the differentiated signifier (i.e., symbol) has been reviewed in chapter 2. From this springboard issues all the further development of theoretical intelligence toward fully coordinated logical operations. While this second phase takes an incomparably longer time span, it is perhaps a less radical logical progression than the achievements of the first two years.

Again in contrast to the contingent character of accommodation, assimilation has a logical—and ultimately a logically necessary—character through which it can be truly constructive and open to newness. There is logic in the development of children, i.e., the making of new connections within and between schemes, as there is logic underlying the developed thinking of adults. Unfavorable emotional or social circumstances can effectively interfere with both development and the logic of adults— and here adult thinking is more vulnerable than child development—but this does not justify the conclusion that social or material circumstances are the source of the logic of knowledge or its development.

Enough has been said on Piaget's biological principle of assimilation to suggest a first approximation between it and Freud's basic life drive or eros. Where Freud attempted a most general description of eros, he used phrases such as "to unify and connect" or "to bring together biological elements into ever widening units." Piaget's description of the principle of assimilation as it works in evolution and development is almost identical to Freud's terminology. It is granted that the two scholars drew different consequences from this common basis, Freud stressing the drive character providing the psychological energy for making the connections and Piaget the logical character inherent in any adaptive connecting. But neither of the two would carry their own viewpoint so far as to exclude the other. This is more obvious in Piaget's case where there are numerous references to assimilatory schemes, which as it were search for objects-to-assimilate and are fueled by them.

A knowledge theory that begins by equating knowledge and biological action cannot but postulate that an organism is equipped with the basic drive to use its action schemes (and in so doing develop its knowledge capacity), even as it assumes there is a logical quality to every action (insofar as it is an active coordinating between organism and environment). While it is thus easy to establish a motive component at the core of Piaget's assimilation model, can we find an analogous knowledge component in Freud's drive model? Certainly not in any explicit fashion, but remember that all three major themes discussed in the previous chapter relate drive to knowledge components. The objects of dream formation, of unconscious fantasy, and of repression directly concern knowledge material. Freud would be inclined to characterize this knowledge as illogical in the sense of being free of any logical constraint and opposed to the logical thinking of adult consciousness. On this specific point, he is clearly at variance with Piaget. The clearest connection between drive and knowledge is, however, Freud's use of the concept of investment. Before discussing this in the following section, it seems opportune to stay with the drives themselves and see how Freud's two drives could be aligned with Piaget's theory.

Death and destruction are words of strong negative connotation, and it is therefore worthwhile to recall that for Freud these are the ultimate consequences of the drive and by no means intended proximate goals. Would it not be possible to retain the opposing direction to the life drive and yet describe the drive in more general terms? I think this can be done along the line of the proposed contrast of openness versus closure. Openness to new possibilities of organism-environment connections is the most salient goal of the life drive. Closure of the organism would be the analogous aim of the opposing drive. But are these two directions necessarily opposed? For Piaget there is no necessary opposition, but a biologically built-in polarization. He can consequently suggest two basic directions as governing the functioning of all organisms: conservation of its biological structure on the one hand and expansion of its action- (or knowledge-) environment compatible with conservation on the other hand.

Piaget frequently referred to these two basic biological tendencies. He considered them well known and generally accepted, needing no further explanation. But the truly innovative twist on Piaget's part was to link these tendencies to knowledge and its development. Both an organism's structure as well as its environment are constituent parts of the knowledge process. The structure itself enables the organism to act knowledgeably on the environment. And the environment is not the physical but, as it should be, the biological environment, and that means, in Piaget's terminology, the "knowable" or "assimilable" environment. Knowledge therefore serves the twin tendencies of conserving the organism's structure and of expanding the assimilable environment.

Consider these two basic drives, one toward closure and conservation, the other toward openness and expansion. Could this polarity be similar to the one between assimilation and accommodation, and is it a polarity of inverse proportionality adding up to a given constant so that the greater the one, the smaller the other? We shall discuss the second question first and for argument's sake assume an affirmative answer. The supposition is not far-fetched, it underlies many popular interpretations of Piaget as well as of Freud. In Freud's case there is the supposed notion of a fixed amount of energy to be distributed between the drive impulses. The stronger the impulses of one drive, the weaker the impulses of the other. In Piaget's model a similar belief is held relative to the relation between assimilation and accommodation, such that an action with "much" accommodation implies proportionally "less" assimilation and vice versa. Learning by rote a poem in a foreign language could be adduced as an example. There is good accommodation to the sound sequence with no corresponding assimilation of the sound pattern to available language schemes. Assimilation and accommodation are therefore not in balance.

However—and this is Piaget's first and main point—knowledge by itself tends toward a balance. Rote knowledge is a distinctly inferior form of knowledge, and its deficiency points precisely in the direction of what is crucial in all knowledge, namely, the assimilation process. Second, even the most primitive rote knowledge always has some component of assimilation, albeit not at a level corresponding to the exigencies of the situation. Recall that what is accommodated are schemes of assimilation. A person's accommodation of schemes to a given object is but the other knowledge side of the person's assimilation of the object to the schemes. In the given example, sensorimotor schemes of sequential hearing and forming words are a minimum prerequisite; without these there could be no rote imitation of words at all.

There is a further consideration. Common sense tells us that a "good" assimilation never interferes with accommodation. On the contrary, a good understanding of a piece of music makes the expert all the more attentive to, and retentive of, every single musical detail. Similarly, a tailor rather than an untutored lay person is much more likely to notice the perceptible particulars of a suit and subsequently reproduce them materially as a copy in cloth or symbolically in drawings or words. In short, assimilation and accommodation, far from being quantitatively or qualitatively opposed polarities, are in fact complimentary. "Much" assimilation and a "good" assimilation as a rule go hand in hand with a similar kind of accommodation, and vice versa. In what way, then, is there a polarity or opposition between these two concepts? Quite simply in the direction of their respective effects. In assimilation the knower puts the imprint of the schemes on the (object of) actions, in accommodation there is the imprint of the object on the (schemes of) actions. Knowledge-in-action is a two-way affair between the agent (subject) and object. There is no other way of conceptualizing this except by a polarity of direction that, however, must not be extended into an opposition of a quantitative or qualitative nature.

Apparently then, assimilation and accommodation cannot be put alongside the basic tendencies, postulated by Piaget, of conservation and expansion respectively. The fact that many interpreters nevertheless do precisely this is a testimony to Piaget's difficult style and to traditional habits unaccustomed to relational thinking. For these interpreters assimilation is the conservative, habitual pole of knowledge as opposed to accommodation as the expansive pole, responsive to newness. I need only add that in this model the problem of newness is effectively sidestepped in that newness is linked to accommodation as the imitation of a model. This mistaken linkage is one major source of misreading Piaget and reflects an attitude toward knowledge acquisition that cannot handle newness except under the camouflage of discovery or copy of something that is already there. In other words, there would be no genuine newness, only the appearance of newness.

I now propose to consider more closely Piaget's conservation-expansion polarity in relation to Freud's two drives. At the beginning of this chapter these drives were provisionally reconceptualized in terms of closure and openness and Freud's eros and Piaget's assimilation principle were aligned. But where in Piaget's theory would we find anything corresponding to the death drive? If we were to postulate the accommodation pole as being similar to the death drive, we would find ourselves in the curious situation of merely reversing the misinterpretation of the previous paragraph.

As we look closer at the closure-openness polarity and reflect on the putative notion of a fixed libidinal energy, it becomes clear that such an interpretation of Freud would effectively lock the organism into a closed system. What was discussed earlier in the area of knowledge—that newness is the most significant (as well as the most difficult to explain) feature of the knowledge process—needs to be extended to the area of energy or motive power. Life is not merely a process of energy exchange subject to the law of enthropy, i.e., the gradual dissipation of energy. It is also, and above all, a process of construction of new energy, a "fulguration," as K. Lorenz (1973) called it. This means that there is not a fixed amount of energy within which life develops, just as there is not a given preexisting reality within which action and knowledge expands.

All this is strikingly germane to Freud's (1920) biological arguments in which he established the constructive nature of the life drive in deliberate contrast to the conservative nature of the death drive. Yet his description of the death drive is singularly meager and negative. It is said to be particularly evident in the compulsive repetitions of traumatic actions. For the rest it is described as unconcerned about the pleasure principle or the reality principle, protective of self against outside influences, unwilling to make new connections, hostile against otherness, aggressive toward the other and ultimately the self. While Freud called it the "destruction" drive, it is to be noted that the German word *"Destruktion"* has a more neutral and psychological association than the same word in the English language, where the physical act of destroying is connoted. In the context of Freud's discussion, *destruction* refers to the breaking down of psychological connections and this is in clear contrast to *eros*, which tends toward the construction of an ever-widening network of psychological connections. Love of the other (in whatever form the other is constituted) and fear for self seem to be the two basic human emotions that correspond most directly to the polarity of Freud's life drive and death drive. In terms of direction, the life drive is constructive and open to the other, the death drive is conservative (or restrictive) and closed on the self.

My aim is still to search within Piaget's theory for an equivalent to Freud's conservation drive after having proposed to link the life drive with the assimilation principle. Now that we have reached the point where we can speak of a conservation drive, we are suddenly reminded that conservation is a significant concept within Piaget's theory. It refers to the knowledge of invariance, notably quantitative invariance, e.g., the understanding that a given amount of liquid in a wide container reaches a proportionally higher level when it is poured into a narrow container. The amount is "conserved" even though size dimensions are dramatically changed. Children around nine years old can justify the conservation as a logically necessary implication from their developed operation of quantity. However, in this model of Piaget there is nothing negative about conservation. On the contrary, it is representative of the balance and stability between assimilation and accommodation toward which knowledge by itself tends.

Quite generally, conservation is linked to the closure of a logical system within which mental operations can move in any direction and return to the starting point. The (logically necessary) understanding of a seven-year-old girl that a grandmother is also a granddaugther and that in a classroom full of children and one teacher there are more people than children are illustrations of the closure of the classificatory system. In chapter 2 the developmental acquisition of the permanent object was discussed and even at this early age (around age two) Piaget attributed to the child, if not a systematic, nonetheless a pre-form of conservation, namely, to mentally conserve an object in space and time, even though it is no longer a present action object. To apply this conservation of a mental object to the conservation of the self, picture logical understanding as a conservation of the thinking self. In making a logical judgment—as a rule habitually and implicitly—you conserve the integrity and consistency of yourself as a thinker.

Now recall that Piaget postulated two basic knowledge tendencies: to conserve the organism and to expand the assimilable environment. These two tendencies as such are not conflicting, although they are clearly different in direction, conservation being self-directed, and expansion outside-directed. What then is their relation? Consider an organism equipped with knowledge schemes (whether instinctual or developmental makes no difference) to build a shelter along the slope of a hill and another organism able to build a shelter not only in this one general topography but in almost any location, on flat ground, in trees, over rocks, near the water. Which of the two has more schemes and which of the two has a more expanded assimilable environment? The answer is obvious, but ponder also that the second organism has a greater measure of autonomous control and more degrees of freedom. All this is in direct proportion to the complexity of knowledge schemes.

Then take architects who use their theoretical knowledge, constrained as it is by the closure of mathematical and logical operations, and ask yourself how the constraints of necessary logical conservation are related to the opening up of indefinite and ever new possibilities. There are some people who see only the constraining side of logic and devaluate it as a lifeless framework that has never produced more than familiar answers. They interpret Piaget's assimilation in this restrictive sense and then need accommodation to explain any new adaptation in knowledge. More consistently, many dismiss the theory as irrelevant They fail to realize that without the constraints of a logical framework human thinking would not be free to produce continually new achievements, whether in science or art or the interpersonal relations and values that hold a society together.

Piaget's theory made explicit that the closure of logical knowledge is a prerequisite for the opening up of theoretical possibilities. He documented (1976b) that frequently what today is judged to be (necessarily) possible, at some earlier time was considered (again, necessarily) impossible. This is as true in individual as in societal knowledge development. The six-year-old child who judges the amount of water to be more in the thin than in the wide beaker: "since it is higher it must be more," a few years later judges quite routinely: "it is and must be higher since it is the same." In the intervening year this child has developed a fully operatory scheme (i.e., operation) of three-dimensional amounts and assimilates the situation to it, whereas the earlier scheme was only partially operatory and focused on the more easily observable two-dimensional quantity of height. At both times the child's knowledge was "in balance." But in-between there must have been some awareness of imbalance, perhaps nothing more than a vague feeling of "there is a gap," "something missing in me as a thinker." This can become the occasion for a reconstruction of the child's schematism, provided always there is the requisite motivation and energy.

What this occasion is would be hard to spell out. Only rarely do children themselves take explicit note of it, as can happen when a new insight is first constructed in the presence of a problem situation set up by an examiner. That quantity as a concept is taught by explicit instruction is not at all likely and moreover would quickly reveal itself as useless. Accommodation is therefore not much in evidence, but the principle of expanding assimilation is at work. The child constructs, or better, reconstructs a scheme of assimilation on a new level and in so doing compensates for the experienced logical insufficiency of the former scheme. In this model of development what can be called the drive for conservation and the drive for expansion go hand in hand: in expanding the assimilable universe, the child at the same time conserves the self as a logical thinker.

But this fortunate state of affairs is more the ideal and the exception than the rule. What if the child had not been motivated to expand the energy of compensating for a gap in understanding and simply suppressed the vaguely experienced insufficiency? What if society discouraged such questions as idle speculations and expected useful work or some other activity as the customary role for nine-year-old children? What if a strong emotional attachment adhered to the earlier scheme or if conversely the specific subject matter—for psychological or physiological reasons—was highly unpleasurable to the child? I list these things to indicate that in the development of knowledge Piaget indeed assumed a constellation of favorable circumstances including energy, motivation, social occasion, a healthy brain. I believe Piaget was justified in making these assumptions, since these con-

ditions invariably prevail in any society, at least for some knowl-
édge areas, and the younger the children the more frequent and
more welcome the occasions of knowledge disturbance and subsequent compensation and knowledge reconstruction.

Moreover, as Piaget's aim was to show the spontaneous base of scientific thinking, he focused on logical-mathematical understanding in as explicit a manner as possible. He
accepted science as one ideal of knowledge but nowhere implied
that it was the only acceptable or indeed suitable model for any
and all human actions. Nevertheless the developmental sequence
of conservation, expansion, disturbance, compensation, reconstruction, conservation is valid for all areas and at all stages of
development. This is one important conclusion for the present
discussion.

Another comment is also pertinent. Where there is
conflict between conservation and expansion, in the end conservation prevails. I will rephrase this sentence more precisely, taking
account of the implicit logic in all development. Knowledge is a
state of balance that tends both to conserve itself and to expand
its assimilable scope; if the expansion is small and does not lead
to a knowledge disturbance, conservation is maintained; if, however, expansion is more substantial and leads to a knowledge
disturbance, the tendency is to compensate for the disturbance by
a reconstruction through which the newly expanded knowledge
is again in a state of balance. If for any reason the reconstruction
is not done, the knowledge disturbance is suppressed and the
former state of balance is reconstituted.

The conservation tendency (of maintaining the self in
balance with the environment) is basic, and the more expanded
the scope of assimilation, the tighter the network of sche nes and
the stronger the conservation tendency. The expansion .endency
needs conservation as a base and aims at restructuring schemes
at a higher level of conservation; this progression involves a
disturbance of the first conservation, of greater or lesser intensity and duration; the reconstruction is therefore at the same
time a compensation for a disturbance. The more expanded
and tighter the network of schemes, the less likely is there a

knowledge disturbance, followed by subsequent compensation and expansion.

> Every differentiation constitutes a new kind of possible disturbance and this in relation to the cohesion of the total cyclic system (of which the subsystem is a part). As a consequence, either the cycle is broken [and there is no development] or the cohesion (as interactions of conservation) exercises its assimilatory power on the differentiated subsystems. In that case, the differentiation is compensated by integration and there is a new and enriching expansion due to equilibration. But this integrative power of the totality is not a *deus ex machina* arising at the occasion without previous work: it is integral to assimilation. (If assimilation is indeed *deus*, it is so in relation not merely to cognitive functions, but to life in general, in all its manifestations.) In fact, any process of assimilation is necessarily cyclic and self-conservative. This is the reason for the resistance of any total system (of whatever rank) to its differentiation and for its compensatory reactions in the form of integration. (1975: 37–38)

This sketch of Piaget's (1975, Furth 1981: ch. 5) equilibration model, if elaborated in sufficient detail, could go some way to explain why all children everywhere do develop and expand their knowledge schemes, whereas after adolescence knowledge development is much more rare and is strongly conditional on specific social conditions and individual differences. It also follows that the relation between these two tendencies cannot be uniquely described. From one perspective they seem to cooperate (as in early childhood); from another, they seem to be in conflict (after adolescence). From yet another perspective, they are complimentary, depending on each other: the schemes that conserve have come into being by expansion, expansion needs conservation as a basis; an organism with schemes that no longer expand will in the long run die.

Reflecting on the last few pages, it is apparent that Piaget's description of the knowledge process, driven by the twin tendencies to conserve and to expand, is not so different from Freud's description of the interplay of eros and death drive. The fact that one can easily observe the workings of the two tendencies in the knowledge development of a child should be seen as an advantage over Freud's model in which the manifestations of the death drive are indeed obscure. I think it is now possible—and for the sake of a true synthesis, required—to end this section with common names for Freud's and Piaget's two basic tendencies. For Freud the life and death drives are closely linked to the emotions underlying human actions. If we accept the saying that a knowledge that does not expand is dead, we could use the same designations and refer to knowledge that is (relatively) alive or dead. But we can be more precise in showing that the two drives are not *logical* opposites, rather they are different and complimentary and only in certain circumstances conflicting.

I suggest two words, *constructive* and *restrictive*, as most appropriate to point to the construction and expansion of life and knowledge on the one hand and to conservation, restriction, and destruction on the other hand. The common link of the two would be the one noun that the adjectives differently modify, and I can think of no better one than the concept of *assimilation*, which specifies the difference between material and biological reality. A drive of *constructive assimilation* would correspond to (Freud's) eros drive and (Piaget's) tendency to expand. A drive of *restrictive assimilation* would be the equivalent to (Freud's) death drive and (Piaget's) tendency to conserve. All life and all knowledge would then be conceptualized as the historical product of the unceasing interplay of the two biological drives of constructive and restrictive assimilation.

It is a dual drive model, as postulated by Freud, with constructive assimilation making all the noise and disturbance as it produces changes and new connections, while restrictive assimilation works more quietly and deeply to maintain and defend the balances of the past. In these rather general terms, whatever in the narrow sense is called knowledge and emotions is fully included. Indeed Piaget's (1975) equilibration model of knowledge development, as sketched in the preceding pages, illustrates the tendencies of the two drives in a somewhat more explicit and comprehensible manner than Freud's biological speculations and illustrative case studies.

Nevertheless, to achieve a meaningful integration of their theories, it does not suffice to point to commonalities underlying the source of development for both knowledge and emotions. After all, these two, certainly for adults, are as a rule quite different psychological realities. It remains to specify in detail the interplay of knowledge and emotions (or drive impulses, to use a terminology more in line with Freud). For the purpose of elucidating this crucial point, there can be no more fruitful approach than to turn to the beginning of children's symbolic activities where the separation of knowledge from emotionally driven actions has its developmental origin.

KNOWLEDGE AS DRIVE INVESTMENT

As repeatedly stressed in previous chapters, with object formation around age two, knowledge is on the threshold of a qualitative change. Symbol formation in its various forms was shown to be a psychological consequence of object knowledge. The three most important symbolic acts are symbolic gestures (e.g., play), symbolic images (e.g., fantasy), and symbolic communication (e.g., language). In a manner quite different than sensorimotor actions, which are constrained and partially determined by present material and social conditions, the first two forms at the least pose a distinct problem of motivation. In chapter 2 we became familiar with Piaget's model of symbol formation. While we noted its unique standing among other theories that use symbols without explicating their psychological origin or function, we realize that Piaget never intended to provide a comprehensive theory of symbol formation including its motivational basis. For that missing component, I turned in chapter 3 to Freud. In it I presented a developmental perspective on three of Freud's major themes, interpreting them to be sure (as one must if one is more than a silent transmitter), but on the whole staying within the theory (as I did for Piaget in chapter 2). In this chapter, however, I deliberately go beyond in an attempt to see the one theory from the viewpoint of the other. In the preceding section I have portrayed Freud's basic drives with the help of Piaget's perspective on knowledge and here I shall attempt to integrate Piaget's symbol theory with Freud's perspective on drive investment.

Freud's German word is *Besetzung* which literally means "occupation," "taking charge"; English-speaking translators have invented the words *cathexis* and *to cathect*, yet another instance where Freud's preference for common terms has been thwarted by misplaced technical specialization. Also note that Freud's early use of the concept leaned heavily on neurological considerations in that nervous energy was thought to be locally invested in particular neurons or nervous constellations. Soon, however, these physiological overtones became less important. From the time psychoanalysis gave up hypnosis as a method and relied entirely on psychological treatment, investment and its surrounding concepts became increasingly the province of a person's psychology (or psyche, as Freud would say). The process itself is straightfordward: the person invests the energy of a drive in objects. Freud called the energy of the sexual drive libido and retained the name when the drive was expanded into the life drive or eros.

At this point I want to focus on the object of investment and state again that English-speaking interpreters of Freud have been seriously sidetracked by the nonpsychological meaning of the English word "object" as a material thing. For Freud, as we know, object never meant a thing as such, but always a psychological object. When I now correlate Freud's object to Piaget's object concept, I follow Freud's own direction and make it psychologically more explicit. We recall from chapter 2 that developmentally the object derives from action knowledge in which it is at first an undifferentiated object of action. Around age two children have developed their knowledge framework to the point that action knowledge can be separated from the present action; this is the origin of the object proper as an object of knowledge. With this as a base, my argument continues: *when the object is invested with libido it becomes a symbol.*

The symbol is the clearest psychological reality where Freud's and Piaget's theories meet, the one supplying the motivation component, the other the knowledge component. To make present an absent reality requires both a knowledge of coordinating signifier and signified and the energy and motivation to construct a new reality. Let there be no doubt about the newness of this construction. The fact that symbolic reality comes about gradually so that by age six and from then onward it literally engulfs human psychology in all its aspects is no reason to neglect the qualitative change from the sensorimotor universe of a two-year-old child to the symbolic universe of a six-year old child. For Freud (1926:14) the symbol is a "drive-representative" (14:132), a "carrier of impulses" (14:118). "A drive cannot become a conscious object, only the symbol representing it. In the unconscious too it cannot be represented in any other way than by a symbol" (Freud 1915c 10:275). Two pages later Freud stated unequivocally that "symbols are investments (basically of memory traces), whereas affects and feelings are discharge processes which are ultimately experienced as emotions" (10:277).

In the last quote, Freud touched upon a characteristic peculiar to symbols that amounts to a separation of affect and symbol even though symbols are originally investments on the part of the drives. In fact, this displacement of affect was one of the first things he noticed in his neurotic clients. "The *hysteric* who weeps at A is quite unaware that he is doing so on account of the association A-B, and B itself plays no part at all in his psychological life. The symbol has in this case taken the place of the *thing* entirely" (1895, 1:349). Whereas B was the original symbol invested by the drive (the "thing"), now a secondary symbol A has taken on the meaning and affect of B.

The separation and displacement of meaning and affect can be considered a special case within the more general separation of action and knowledge that enables symbol formation in the first place. Note that any symbol of whatever form implies a primary displacement of affect in that the symbol by definition is separated from its appropriate concrete object of action. Consequently, the affect toward that object can be said to be displaced from the object of action to the object of knowledge. Before the separation, any action has its appropriate range of knowledge and emotion without which the action would not take place. This is most conspicuous in instinctual actions, but it is also the case in sensorimotor actions. An eleven-month-old girl who otherwise loves to crawl back and forth through a tunnel will not do so when she is emotionally attuned to interacting with a newly arrived playmate.

However, after action separation a drive impulse, instead of being attached to and discharged by a present action, can attach itself to an imaginary (possible) action by providing the energy to form a symbol. What is the state of these imaginary actions? On the material (perhaps also neurological) side they are former accommodations (familiar movements), on the meaning side they are part of the child's assimilatory knowledge (schemes). But this Piagetian description of the symbolic state omits the crucial contribution of the drive impulse that provides the child's knowledge apparatus with the energy to form the symbol. From a psychological perspective the symbolic object, unlike the present object, has no physical (action), but only a psychological connection to the symbolizer. As a consequence, although there is an appropriate drive impulse at the action origin of the symbol, another drive impulse is behind the present symbol construction and it is possible that the present affect is no longer appropriate to the original impulse.

Freud realized that in the course of development the quality of energy investment changes. His comments on it are quite frequent but by no means consistent or systematic. I am referring here to the contrast of free and bound energy. I would like to discuss this contrast along with the emergence of the "I" (ego and narcissism), another area where Freud's own writing shows internal inconsistencies. Consider infants prior to the achievement of the symbolic capability. As pointed out earlier, their action world is bounded by present material and social constraints. In this respect sensorimotor development during the first two years is a steady progression in the knowledge of the present world of senses and movements. This is the phase where, as Freud

(1915a 10:228) says, "a primitive reality-ego has differentiated inside and outside [of the body] by means of valid objective criteria." Freud aptly referred to this as a "body ego," a phrase that could be improved by calling it an "action ego." In another remarkable paper, Freud noted:

> all internal images derive from perception, are repetitions of perceptions. Initially the existence of a perceptual representation guaranteed the reality of what is represented. The opposition between subjective and objective does not exist in the beginning. It comes about only insofar as thinking acquires the capacity through representative reproduction to make again present something previously perceived while the outside object need no longer be there. The first and most direct purpose of reality testing is therefore, not to find in real perception an object corresponding to the image, but to regain it, to feel convinced it is still there. Another factor of alienation between subjective and objective is due to another capability of thinking. The image reproduction of a perception is not always a faithful repetition; it can be modified by omission or changed by fusion of different elements. Reality testing has then to control the extent of these distortions. One recognizes as a precondition for initiating reality testing that objects have been lost which once provided real satisfaction. (1925 14:14)

Here again, as before, Freud refers to an initial state of undifferentiation. The possibility of being alienated from reality by a thinking that separates the subject from the object of the action does not yet exist. Symbolic reproduction, however, can picture for real what does not exist and can "lie." Why would a biologically sound organism bother with such unrealities? Freud's laconic answer, to regain lost objects of the past, is but another way of saying that the energy of infantile libidinal impulses is invested in these symbols and thereby they become emotionally real and meaningful.

As an aside note the similarity between Piaget and Freud in their description of the image capacity, all the more striking considering that Freud was little concerned about a knowledge theory. Yet how much more careful is Freud in his use of representative and reproductive images than more recent interpreters. As suggested before, there are many who uniformly attribute even to the youngest infants the power to fantasize and form images of absent realities, a power that according to Piaget is not present nor required in sensorimotor knowledge: sensorimotor recognition is not image memory but present familiar accommodation.

The ego changes that Freud in the preceding quote attributed to the newly acquired symbol function refer to reality testing, a task that (as Piaget shows) is well beyond the power of children before age six to seven. Without the closure of mental operation, reality testing is at best partial and uncertain. Nevertheless, symbol formation as subject-object separation makes reality testing imperative; this need calls forth the motivation to construct operations through which the children can eventually put some measure of order into their fantasies and can distinguish what is subjective and what is objective (real).

But for the time being the ego's primary concern is not socialized reality but pleasure. At first the primitive action ego turns into a pleasure ego: "The primal reality-ego which has differentiated inside and outside by objective criteria is changed into a purified pleasure ego which values pleasure above all" (Freud 1915a 10:228). Here Freud spelled out the distortions that symbol formation makes possible. Whatever is pleasure is introjected and assimilated to the ego; whatever is displeasure is projected and assimilated to the outside world. The phrase "purified pleasure" was chosen by Freud to distinguish it from a previous state where what he called the "displeasure" principle was at work (namely, avoidance of pain). Note well that the avoidance of displeasure is something quite different from the subsequent active search for pleasure combined with interest in the "other" (in contrast to a previous "indifference").

As the following quote will show, Freud considered it the primary task of earliest infancy to bind the stimulation reaching the psychological apparatus without which the pleasure principle cannot operate. This task of binding, principally attributed to the conservation drive, would make it possible for the eros drive to flourish and expand. Consider Freud's delicate distribution of tasks: the conservation drive does the binding, but the eros drive provides the material to be bound. Binding the energy of eros would permit pleasure (libido) to become an object, an object of knowledge and of desire. A developmental transition leads therefore from random to bound drive energy, from the sway of restrictive assimilation (conservation drive) to constructive assimilation (eros drive), from the principle of avoiding displeasure to the active search for pleasure, from indifference to interest in the other as a psychological "object."

> It would be the task of the higher layers of the psychological apparatus to bind the excitation drives reaching the primary processes. Failure to bind would cause a disturbance somewhat like a traumatic neurosis; only after successful binding would the power of the pleasure principle (and its modification as reality principle) be uniformly established. Until that time the other task of the psychological apparatus, namely to control and bind the excitation, would be foremost, a task not necessarily opposed to the pleasure principle, but apart from it and in part unconcerned about it. (Freud 1920 13:36)

My contention is that the "primal" binding of libidinal energy takes the form of investments in symbols (images) of precisely those objects to which the child is emotionally attached. Within this world of symbols, the pleasure principle reigns supreme. In symbol formation, as Piaget has shown, the children assimilate reality to their personal pleasure. This sentence can be turned around to say: the children in forming symbols construct their personal pleasure reality. The libidinal investment in this reality is not inward directed to the self—a common misinterpretation of Piaget's term *egocentric.* On the contrary, the pleasure is object-directed, and this implies a strong personal attachment to others.

In chapter 3, I paraphrased this symbol world as "want-my-object." Note the absence of an "I" to whom egocentrism could be attributed. It should be added that the children are constantly constructing new objects by relating to them in different situations in terms of emotions, particular actions, new combinations, etc. In short, the accent is on assimilation (free of reality constraints), pleasure in objects, newness, construction. The energy for this comes from the eros drive, the vehicle for it is the symbol, the interest is in the object, and the psychological work is a socially unconstrained constructive assimilation (Piaget) or a primary process (Freud).

Confusion arises relative to the binding of libidinal energy. The more usual reference to free versus bound energy is parallel to the contrast of primary and secondary process or pleasure principle and reality principle. In the primary system there is "free discharge of the quantities of excitation while the second system through its investments produces a control of discharge so that there is a change to a stable investment along with a rise of its action potential" (Freud 1900 2-3:605). In contrast to the free discharge of primary investments, there is the "stable investment" of thinking that "can be considered a rehearsal action, a motor trial with small discharge of quantities. . . The function of judgment becomes successful only after the construction of the negation symbol provides thinking with a first degree of independence from the products of repression and with it, from the constraints of the pleasure principle (1925 15:14–15)."

If you compare this with previous quotes, you note the apparent inconsistencies that have puzzled interpreters. Here a binding of excitation in the stable investments of thinking leads to freedom from the pleasure principle and thereby to the psychology of secondary processes and of the reality principle. Earlier it was said that the binding of excitation establishes the pleasure principle in the first place and that as a consequence reality testing needs to be initiated.

To resolve this difficulty I have already suggested that the early binding be referred to as primal. It begins around age two in the form of object and symbol formation. The objects are the interpersonal relations in which the little children find themselves, and the affective energy of these objects is "bound" in the symbols. While this new psychological acquisition allows the children to construct a symbolic reality alongside the continuing action reality, it does not yet provide them with the controls to put order into the chaos of their symbol world. Here then is Freud's oedipal world where the "want-my-object" principle holds sway, only marginally checked by a tentative and inconsistent reality testing. In this mental world, the pleasure ego easily prevails over the action ego. There is chaos for lack of order in emotions or knowledge, both of them separated for the first time from the reality constraints of action. Yet without action separation there would be no personal emotions or theoretical knowledge at all.

The emotional chaos typified by the mobility of affect and the free discharge of libidinal energy frequently spills over into the action world of the little ones. Its substance is subject to primal repression. Later on when the reality principle permits a clear discrimination between image and reality, the emotional chaos does at times erupt into action and consciousness—in fantasies and dreams, in neurotic or psychotic actions of individuals or groups—and Freud's description of the unconscious id is still the best characterization. That the symbolic knowledge of little children is severely distorted by the unconstrained attitude of the pleasure principle and their lack of a developed logical system is amply documented by Piaget's works. It can be easily observed by anyone who looks behind young children's volatile behavior and unpredictable playfulness in their actions and conversations.

Piaget discovered the establishment of the first logical systems of thinking—he called it concrete operations—around the age of five to seven years, the same age at which Freud postulated that children give up their oedipal world. Again, both knowledge and emotions are at a momentous threshold. The emotional world that eros and the pleasure principle built is given up and the logical operations for the first time introduce logical necessity and justified reason into the children's psychology. The children have by now achieved the emotional maturity to invest their libido in the wider reality beyond their homes and are excited to use for this purpose the logical operations they are constructing. At this point there is a second binding of libido and symbolic object, which in contrast to the earlier chaotic and my-want-oriented symbolic world leads to a more ordered and socially shared world. It is still a world of symbols—language, science, art, ideals, values—but shared symbols that are the fabric of our human socialized reality. In this sense Freud refers to the reality principle and the stable investments of secondary process psychology.

The following is a schematic outline of a developmental progression where the difference between the primal and secondary binding is made explicit.

Age	Ego	Logic	Libido	Discharge	Process	World
0–2	Action	Action (sensori-motor)	Free	—	Avoidance of pain	Action
2–6	Pleasure	Object, Symbol (pre-operatory)	Bound	Free	Primary	Private symbolic
6+	Reality	Operations	Bound	Controlled	Secondary	Socialized symbolic

In the first two years the infant's psychology is driven by openness to the action world, the primary action being participation in the satisfying context of interpersonal relations. Libido is freely expended—and therefore does not need to be discharged—in whatever actions happen to be available. Conservation (survival) of the individual is assured by the psychological process of avoidance of displeasure.

In contrast, in two- to six-year-old children libidinal impulses are beginning to be bound (primal binding) and invested in symbols. Through these symbolic investments the displeasure-avoiding action ego is becoming a pleasure-seeking symbolizing ego. The investments are logically and emotionally unstable as the children are largely unconcerned about logical consistency or the wider social reality. Analogously, the affects bound in the symbols are freely displaced and discharged. The private world constructed in these symbols is, in Freud's language, the Oedipus fantasy. Primary process psychology and a not-yet-socialized ego are at work.

The second binding of libidinal energy of which Freud speaks is displayed at the third level and refers to a more controlled discharge of affect connected with the already symbol-bound libidinal impulses. As before, there are emotional and knowledge preconditions. The children must feel sufficiently secure in their action reality to let go of the objects of their private symbolic world (primal repression) and open up toward the wider world of others. But in order to share with others, especially peers, and clearly discriminate between private and social reality, logical operations are needed that rest on the firm basis of logical necessity. Under these conditions a stable investment of drive impulses in socially shared symbols is possible. This implies a corresponding modification and control of the pleasure principle and of free (i.e., self-oriented) discharge of affect. The result is the construction of a socialized world by the secondary process psychology of the reality ego.

It remains to add that libidinal investment in the symbol world does not do away with a person's action world. We should think of the private symbolic world as gradually being added onto the ongoing and enlarging world of sensorimotor actions and having increasingly significant repercussions on it. A four-year-old-child with a well-developed pleasure ego still is, or has, an action ego. Without the action ego there would be no further growth in knowledge since the unmodified pleasure principle, free of social or logical constraints, is hardly conducive to development. Paradoxically then, libidinal investments in symbols are at first the occasion of an apparent detour in development, even a kind of regression. Children between ages two to six have to reconstruct a framework of logical regulations on the symbolic level and start again almost from zero, even though they have already progressed considerably on the sensorimotor level. Thus symbol formation is both an emotional and a knowledge investment, yet the primary task of this childhood period has more to do with emotions than with knowledge as such.

To take a trivial example, think of three-year-old children playing car. On the sensorimotor action level, they know perfectly well that they cannot walk up a wall or on the ceiling without immediately falling to the ground. In playing and symbolic fantasy, however, they delight in moving an imaginary car in just these positions. You can say self-oriented wishes prevail over understanding, emotions over knowledge. Do they really not know or do they merely pretend not to know? As far as the children's attitude is concerned, the question is beside the point. They are interested in constructing their own reality; they do not really care for knowledge. And if they did, they would lack the instruments to distinguish between what is possible in imagined self-oriented fantasy and in reality-oriented images. The operations beginning to be achieved around age six are precisely those instruments of knowledge that will place children in a position to put some logical order into their symbolic world: now it is knowledge over emotions, or better, knowledge supported by emotions. The detour is ended and knowledge development proceeds apace.

What a strange history! Why this roundabout progress? What is the meaning of having to build a distorted symbolic world that in the end has to be discarded and repressed? The following chapters are devoted to explore this issue.

Interlude:
Preliminary Summary

Prior to extending the inquiry into areas further afield it may be opportune to summarize now in brief outline the Freudian-Piagetian synthesis achieved in the preceding chapters.

OBJECT AND SYMBOL FORMATION

In continuous knowledge development from birth, infants around age two achieve a new logical stage of knowing: the capacity to understand action situations as objects of knowledge and to make these objects psychologically present in symbolic representations. The three chief forms of symbolic acts (or simply, symbols) are symbolic gesture and play, language as symbolic social communication, and internal symbolism or mental imagery. These new achievements are the developmental results of expanding sensorimotor actions, specifically the increasing differentiation of assimilation and accommodation. The assimilation relation is the psychological source of the experience of the agent, the "I"; the accommodation relation on the other hand leads to the experience of resistance on the part of another, an "object." Both relations or directions, in varying degrees of focus and differentiation, are always simultaneously present. As sensorimotor knowledge is present action, the two-directional relation is between an agent and another person or thing. The new developmental achievements usher in a new type of knowledge, one that can be separated from present action, hence its name of theoretical or representative knowledge. It too implies a mutual relation of an "I" (who knows) to an object (that is known). In symbol formation accommodation provides the symbolic material, assimilation the symbolic meaning.

LIBIDO INVESTED IN OBJECTS AND SYMBOLS

The modern concept of object has been depersonalized and value-neutralized to the extent that it has become synonymous with a factual thing. However, a thing has nothing to do with psychology or with knowledge, unless it is somehow acted upon; and every action implies an agent, the capacity to act (i.e., to assimilate and to accommodate) and the motivation and energy to act. For biological and sensorimotor actions, the motivation is rather directly related to the given ecological situation. The principles of expanding assimilation (libido) and avoidance of pain (survival) are at work. With symbolic actions, however, this direct connection is no longer available since the motivating component is not in the material situation as such but in the symbolic meaning given to it by the "I". The problem is: Why would children *want* to symbolize, what do they get out of it? Clearly Piaget's description of object and symbol formation needs to be completed by an energizing motor beyond the general drive to assimilate and expand the assimilable world, implicitly assumed in his theory. Here I accept Freud's insight that the energy of one of the most potent biological drives—libido—is linked to the formation of objects and symbols. Note that the objects of little children are not just things-out-there, but primarily the social relations to their caretakers, involving most intense emotions of various and frequently conflicting sorts. Hence symbol formation as the reenactment of libidinal investments gives rise to a new form of organism-context relations, namely personal relations, and it serves the purpose of binding libidinal pleasure in mental products.

PLEASURE PRINCIPLE AND EROS DRIVE

Since symbolic objects are constrained neither by other people, external reality, nor by internal logic, the construction of a mental world in the form of symbols is at first entirely under the sway of the pleasure principle. "Want-my-object" would be an apt articulation of young children's symbolism. Nevertheless, the focus is on the object, not on the "I" which is only just beginning to be experienced as a separate self. Thus the pleasure is in the other, not in the self, even though at first the other is known only in a radically asocial, egocentric way. Eros drive is Freud's name for the general tendency to be open to others, to welcome the newness of objects and to expand the desirable world. This drive, which is present to a limited extent in all biology, becomes an explosive force in human psychology with its long individual development and its open-ended, unlimited openness in constructing social and cultural reality.

CLOSURE PRINCIPLE
AND DEATH DRIVE

An unlimited biological openness can never be absolute, only relative. To the eros drive must correspond an equally basic drive to closure or conservation of the organism. Freud called it the death drive and linked it to aggression and destruction, first against others, ultimately against self. In terms of primary emotions, eros means love of others, death drive fear for self. In combination the two drives provide the motivational energy to maintain and develop the organism. The interaction of the opposing drives implies conflict, tension, ambivalence, compromise. In knowledge, as in emotions, there is a constant tension between "fight or flight" versus "mate or make." In Piaget's language eros corresponds to constructive assimilation, the drive to incorporate, to expand, and to construct newness—in whatever form. To the death drive corresponds a different form of assimilation, restrictive assimilation that closes up a person from the influence of others. During childhood the eros drive and its libidinal constructive assimilations are particularly dominant, hence the universality of childhood development, in contrast to the much slower and rarer progress of further adult development, whether individually or socially. Human knowledge, like interpersonal relations (of which it is both a precondition, a component part, and a co-constructive result), is something alive and cannot stand still. Therefore expansion of knowledge is not something merely added from outside. The logical operations, though they are in themselves mechanisms of logical closure, provide the necessary anchor which grounds the infinite openness of human knowledge, as shown in evolving society, culture, art and science.

PRIMAL REPRESSION
AND THE UNCONSCIOUS ID

Around age six, the time that the closure of the first logical operations is achieved, another closure is about to be completed. It concerns the private symbolic world of childhood, constructed between the ages two to six, according to the children's own desires (pleasure principle) and their limited knowledge. Alluding to the ambivalent emotions toward their parents, dramatized in the Oedipus myth, Freud called it the oedipal world.

While its construction is the outstanding achievement of the eros drive, its final destruction around age six is a manifestation of the drive to defend and conserve and takes the form of a primal repression. As a result the oedipal world lives on in each person's psychology but is no longer available to consciousness. It forms the content of what Freud called the unconscious id and remains almost unchangeable throughout a person's life, in contrast to the new consciousness of the ego, now achieving for the first time the closure of operations. The id is the great reservoir of unconscious drive energy indispensible for achieving mature social and inter-personal relations and the constructive (i.e., expanding) use of human knowledge in its different forms. The id in itself is neither good nor bad—it is an integral part of human psychology and in part (never entirely) explains whatever humans are doing, the best and the worst. Although the id as a whole functions in an unconscious manner, its derivatives can break through into the preconscious and conscious ego, as happens normally in dreams, fantasies, artistic productions, and in all personal-social relations as well as in special cases of psychological dysfunctions or abnormalities (secondary repression).

CONSCIOUSNESS, LOGIC, AND THE SOCIALIZED EGO

Experience of logical necessity is the psychological side of the closure of logical operations. It introduces a new stage of knowing and consciousness, namely the stage of explicit logical operations (Piaget's concrete and formal operations). Along with primal repression and the formation of the id, the ego is established in conscious openness to the wider social world beyond the parental home. The pleasure principle is modified into the reality principle, where reality means primarily social reality. As the unconscious id is heir to the private symbolism (symbolic play and fantasy) of the child, the conscious ego derives from shared sensorimotor and preoperatory actions along with the child's shared symbolism (language, rule games). Sharing is a positive personal relating of "I" to others and vice versa; it includes libidinal components of affect and logical components of coordination (of viewpoints). While primal repression frees the ego's emotions to be attached to social norms, the logical operations at the same time enable the ego to be autonomous and morally (i.e., socially) responsible.

The psychology summarized in these six points is based on my reading of the works of Piaget and Freud. Even though I am aware that my exposition is frequently quite different from that of other interpreters, I am reasonably confident that my interpretation can be justified as being fully consistent with the spirit of the primary authors. The frequent quotes from the original should, if need be, underscore this point. As I turn in the following chapters to areas further away from the psychological field, I freely admit the speculative character of some of the arguments. Readers will realize that two empirical problems approached in the next three chapters are as yet far from closed, with most of the evidence not yet in. I refer here to the history of humanization and the mechanism of biological evolution. Two other problems, namely the reality and source of logical necessity and of moral norms, are frankly philosophical, and any attempt toward solving these problems is bound to be greatly dependent on personal attitudes.

In chapter 5 human knowledge is depicted as having evolved primarily as an adaptation to, and in response to, interpersonal relations. Sexuality in higher animals has already introduced a limited genetic openness in choice of mates and power relations and as such can be seen as contributing towards further evolution in the direction of sociability. In humanization sexuality, fully separated from instinctual actions, has become the motive force in the co-construction of personal relations; in particular, as suggested in the preceding Freud-Piaget synthesis, action-separated libido is the motive side of the coin of action-separated object knowledge. Human childhood is the obligatory developmental phase for the preconscious and unconscious base on which adult personal and societal relations are built.

In chapter 6 symbol formation is then assumed to be the basic psychological construction underlying interpersonal reality as an end in itself. Logical operations, on the other hand, can be said to develop in response to the need to socially coordinate this symbolic knowledge. In fact, theoretical "objective" (means-end) knowledge is grounded in these two mutually related factors: logical operations and social cooperation. Logical necessity implied in the operations is also the prerequisite to the limitless openness of human knowledge development. To the question of how logic entered biology in the first place, Piaget suggests that logic is inadequately conceptualized as the contingent product of evolutionary history. Rather the historical process of evolution itself must be seen as subject to both openness to contingencies and to necessary logical coordination. In this perspective the logical necessity of human psychology derives directly from the logic implicit in all biological assimilation.

Finally, in chapter 7 the operations are shown to belong to the self only insofar as the self is socialized into the community of other "knowers" who are respected on a equal level. All morality and in particular the moral use of operations is predicated on an implicit intention of belonging to the community of persons. This intention, however, requires the personal libido and commitment that in childhood motivated symbol formation in the first place.

In an essay such as this one which leads to the conclusion that all objective knowledge is necessarily linked to subjective unconscious fantasy and desires, I need not be apologetic about introducing matters, not so much for the sake of empirical evidence as for the sake of aesthetic completeness. What follows will probably not convince those who are not already well along the way; but those readers who find the preceding summary meaningful will be helped, as I was, by considering the psychology of knowing in the wider context of evolution and the philosophy of knowledge.

5.

Symbols: The Key to Humanization

IN CHAPTER 2 object- and symbol-formation was depicted as a developmental acquisition that builds on and prolongs the knowledge of sensorimotor actions and carries it beyond the action threshold into the realm of action-separated psychology. At this juncture, around age two, action-separated or theoretical knowledge comes into its own; yet children at this age lack even the most rudimentary regulations appropriate to this new knowledge capability. As a natural consequence, the only guidelines in the construction of this new psychological world are their own as yet barely developed egos with the individual bodily dispositions and action habits. These were acquired in the course of sensorimotor interactions with their caretakers. Behind the weak egos, there are, however, emotions (or affects) of great intensity and, by this time, not only of considerable diversity but also of seriously conflicting tendencies. The same object is loved as well as feared and hated, is desperately approached as source of comfort and at other times just as determinedly pushed away "to let me do it myself." In fact, the children are not at all sure this person who is loved at one time and feared at another, is the same object. While in emotionally relaxed situations they may show their knowledge of the permanence of objects, in emotionally more complex or conflicting situations it will take still a long time before the children have what M. Mahler (1975) calls emotional object constancy.

In chapters 3 and 4, Freud's teaching on infantile wishes underlying the symbolic world of dreams and fantasy was reviewed and interpreted toward discovering the motivational base behind all symbolic activities. Piaget's drive of constructive and expanding assimilation was equated with Freud's eros drive, even as Freud's death drive was linked to conservation or restrictive assimilation. Symbol formation could then be regarded as an emotional as much as a knowledge activity; it satisfies the constructive direction of unifying eros at the same time as it expands assimilation.

The thought occurs: would it be far-fetched to focus on this symbolic function as the fountainhead from which arises the biological uniqueness of human psychology just as developmentally it is the springboard of all further individual development? This would not be the first time that symbolization would be put forward as a species-typical achievement. But when it was done, symbolization was severely restricted to its knowledge component. In the present context, however, symbol formation has a much more inclusive meaning. It means nothing more or less than the separation of sexuality from its heretofore universal function of procreation and the rearing of the young and the investment of this freed sexual energy towards the construction of a symbolic world.

Symbols without libido are of little avail. They simply are not the real thing. It is trivial to argue whether or not the gesture language of the chimpanzee Washoe or other trained primates is truly symbolic and not merely sensorimotor signal communication. That primates communicate and in some fashion, depending on your definitions, come close to object permanence and symbolic understanding are undisputed observations. But equally clear is the decisive fact that primates show no inclination of investing their sexuality in symbols. As a consequence, while for the human child language acquisition is part of the beginning of psychosexuality, that is, free sexuality tied to action-separated psychology, for the chimpanzees it is a matter of learned content that affects their sexuality in no way. What in humans necessarily leads to sexual and logical maturity and its repercussions on interpersonal and societal relations has no counterpart in our evolutionary cousins.

However, it is one thing to assert that an individual developmental history is a prerequisite for mature sexuality (Freud) and logical operations (Piaget). But what evidence can I adduce to back up the statement that the evolutionary process of humanization took the same route? For this is clearly the preceding paragraphs' implication. Evidence in this case can only be indirect and inferential. It would be foolish indeed to use developmental psychology to "prove" the progress of evolution. Nevertheless, both evolution and development are biological processes and can justifiably be said to be constructive of newness. If in development the link of sexuality and object knowledge ushers in the new psychological person, would it not seem reasonable to look for the origin of this link in the changed structures of sexuality and knowledge, characteristic of the earliest form of human life?

A strikingly similar opinion was voiced by the last great down-to-earth philosopher who was also a great scientist and knew the limits of instrumental, scientific knowledge. Speculating on the beginnings of human history, Kant wrote some 200 years ago:

> Humans soon found out: that sexual attraction, which in animals is solely based on temporary, mostly periodic impulses, for them could be made more prolonged and even more intense through the image ability. This ability works on the one hand more moderately but at the same time more permanently and consistently the more the object is withdrawn from the senses. . . . Denial was the contrivance to pass from sensual to mental attraction, from mere animal desire gradually to love, and with this from the feeling of the pleasant to the taste for beauty, first in persons, subsequently also in nature. (1786, 6:89)

HUMAN PSYCHOLOGY ADAPTED
TO PERSONAL RELATIONS

The inquiry into the evolutionary newness of humans would stand on an infinitely more solid footing if agreement could be reached as to what it is to which evolution has adapted the human species. This question is most pertinent as regards the human brain considered as the biological instrument of human knowledge. What is its primary biological function? In response to which problems did it expand into its human form? To this ethologist's question it is appropriate to hear the reply of one of them.

N. K. Humphrey (1976) was dissatisfied with the usual answer that the main role of the primate brain and intellect lies in practical invention relative to the physical environment, such as discovering new ways of doing things and the fabrication of tools. The evidence of the day-to-day life of primates seemed to contradict the image of an active intelligent life. Apart from rare and somewhat artificial occasions, primates, including the immediate ancestors of early humans, established a lifestyle of hunting and gathering "in which, for a period of perhaps ten million years, they could afford to be not only physically but *intellectually* lazy." But then would not this statement constitute a flagrant contradiction to the most basic evolutionary principle of survival value? What is the primate intellect for if it is not the discovery of instrumental knowledge?

In this regard Humphrey pointed to the social life of the primates. It affords both a medium for the cultural transmission of a wide array of subsistence and social strategies and a protective environment for individual learning and development. In his words, "the chief role of the creative intellect is to hold society together." Observing a group of eight or nine chimpanzees in an otherwise barren cage, he "suddenly saw the scene with new eyes . . . these monkeys *had each other* to manipulate and to explore. There could be no risk of their dying an intellectual death when the social environment provided such obvious opportunity for participating in a running dialectical debate." The primate brain seemed to him to "have evolved as an adaptation to the complexities of social living." The survival principle is of course not set aside. Rather, evolution seemed to have reached the point where a long period of childhood, free of survival pressures, and the bonding of younger to older generations indirectly increased the survival potential. "For better or worse," Humphrey concluded, "styles of thinking which are primarily suited to social problem-solving color the behavior of man and other primates even towards the inanimate world."

This evolutionary direction, I submit, continued and took a quantum jump in humans.

> With the transition of *Australopithecus* into *Homo* the most exciting and most unexpected thing in the entire evolution of living matter happened. This was the emergence of conceptual awareness of social forms, the conceptualization of social relations and the prodigious effort to classify ongoing behavior. . . . The emergence of man was essentially a coming into self-awareness of what was already a highly complex social being, and I think that this coming into conceptual awareness was the crucial and fundamental adaptation that enabled man to master first the savanna environment and later the rest of the world. By it he was enabled to achieve a quite rigid and regular pattern of social relations without resorting to the face-to-face system of a baboon-like society. This was man's key adaptation to the open country: the conscious ordering of social relations by conceptualization of the self and of the group, its structure and roles. . . . The best brains in *Homo erectus* probably did not go in for either stone or fire workings . . . rather on something that left no trace—on sociology . . . it is precisely the conceptualizing of existing social relations and the formulating of them using symbolic "tools," e.g., words, that mark the true transition from prehuman ancestor to man. . . . Thus over the millenia man has shaped and constructed his society. He has himself created the immediate matrix of values and norms in which we live. (Reynolds 1976:57–65)

The important point of the anthropologist's argument needs to be underlined, namely, that conceptualization did not create the social forms; the highly complex social communities of the higher apes were already present. Conceptualization, Reynolds asserts, made possible a symbolic relating and a symbolic ordering that no longer depended on face-to-face contact. But what precisely is this concept and symbol capability by which humans are said to construct the self and the social group? As compelling as I find the proposition that social relations are the primary task to which the human brain is adapted, nevertheless I am not satisfied with using adult conceptual thinking or language as a causal explanation for the specific quality of human social relations. These achievements are, of course, an integral part of adult human relations, but they require an explanation as much as human society.

When K. Lorenz (1973) in his essay on the natural history of human knowledge listed seven sources of conceptual thinking, readers should be impressed by the pre-forms of biological intelligence in terms of perceptual abstraction, optical orientation, content learning and memory, voluntary movement, curiosity, imitation, tradition. But to put forward the thesis that the human concept capacity is the integration of these seven things and came into being by an evolutionary fulguration is not at all helpful in understanding the stated uniqueness of humans. Lorenz showed in how many different ways human knowledge is comparable to pre-human forms—supporting Piaget's claim that there is logic in biological actions—and all agree that there are forms of communication and tradition in higher animals.

But where is the decisive difference? I am not asking for a conceptual difference, like Lorenz's integration and fulguration. These are by necessity arbitrary and incomplete. The list of seven things could look differently and have more or fewer items. Rather I am asking a much more concrete question, namely, what could conceivably have happened in the daily lives of our human ancestors that was new and different? Like Marshack (1972) who studied the early roots of civilization, I am dissatisfied with "suddenlies": it is inconceivable that on a certain day, say half a million years ago, a group of humans started out of nowhere to think conceptually and engage in verbal conversation.

But is this not an unreasonable demand comparable to the request of theologians who wanted to know at what point during pregnancy God infused the immortal soul into the growing organism? Not at all. This is no esoteric question but something familiar to anybody concerned with development. There are no "suddenlies" in individual development either; but that does not hinder the ordinary person to accept genuine newness and qualitative differences. (I say ordinary person because some sophisticated scholars all but deny this.) "However far back one goes into history or pre-history, the child has always preceded the adult," said Piaget (1945:211), the first radical developmentalist in the matter of human knowledge. Childhood equals individual development (in contrast to pre-programmed action coordinations), and *childhood and what it implies is as good a candidate as any for being the observable concrete difference that sets humans apart from other animals.*

This is not to say that there is no childhood in many, indeed in most higher animals. But it is severely limited in scope and duration. It stays within the substages of sensorimotor development. Only rarely does it last beyond sexual maturity. Moreover, while curiosity and playful exploration are typical of the childhood of all higher animals, these tendencies become abruptly weaker or disappear altogether when animals reach sexual maturity (Lorenz 1973:276). And there is another significant factor related to childhood and the human condition. Not only is human childhood exceptionally long and productive of the widest scope of developmental acquisitions, the whole human species as a whole is in important respects "childlike." LaBarre (1954) referred to this condition of remaining young as "neoteny" both in anatomical features (e.g., late-closing human skull) and in action patterns, such as the (symbolically and emotionally) permanent belonging to the family and the group and the indefinite openness and playfulness long after sexual maturity.

If sexual maturity triggers the end of childlike attitudes in all but the human species, it follows that changes in sexuality should be as conspicuous as changes in the nature of childhood development. The most obvious is the freeing of sexuality from the biological ovulation cycle. This, together with some anatomical changes due to the upright position, enabled human sexual activity to become something radically different from instinct-dominated action coordinations. Recent views of anthropologists surveying the fossil evidence of early humans accord women's sexuality and childrearing a much more active role than has been customary in a male-dominant perspective. According to one of them (Fisher 1982), female reproductive strategies and female selection of partners on the basis of cooperation between male and female became a driving force in human evolution. This cooperation included the joint rearing of the young. Another innovation highlighting the subordination of instinct in favor of personal social relations was the sharing of plant food, that is, carrying it to one communal eating place rather than consuming it on the spot.

　　If sociability was indeed the primary "function" of the evolving primate brain and intellect, humanization becomes comprehensible as a further specialization or intensification in the same direction. This intensification, I propose here, came about along with a change in knowledge and in sexuality. The first change concerned object knowledge, perhaps nothing more than a dim awareness that "there is a world of other people out there and that I am part of that world." This knowledge would hardly qualify as a "conceptualization" in any adult sense of a logical and articulated concept. Yet it makes possible or rather, it is a prerequisite to a social relation for which the adjective "personal" is appropriate. For the "objects" of the budding intellect are persons toward which I, also being a person, have strong feelings. These are not static mental objects, like definitions or descriptions in a book; they are other persons with whom I interact, just as the self is dimly recognized as the active person on this side of that other person. If this is what Reynolds, quoted earlier, means by conceptualization, I can follow him. I see here the evolutionary breakthrough from action relations to personal relations; in a sense it is the birth of the person.

　　But this is only half of the story and, if weights have to be given, the lesser half. The freeing of knowledge from present action would be pointless unless the organism at the same time cared to invest energy in this new object knowledge. The bursting of the instinct, suggested above, relates primarily to the freeing of knowledge, and Piaget and Lorenz used the object notion in this sense. But clearly, instinctual action is always tied to biological instinctual energy. Freeing of knowledge must then go hand in hand with freeing of energy.

The reproductive instinct throughout the animal species is fairly rigidly tied to instinctual action-coordinations covering the whole cycle of selection, pair formation, nest building, mating, birth, rearing, and protection of the young. All these actions are under the tight control of the sexual instinct, even in higher animals where there is some degree of freedom and individual choice in selection of the mate. Considering the necessity of conserving the species, evolution apparently could not afford to grant more freedom in knowledge and investment of instinctual energy. Nevertheless, the window of freedom was, as we have seen, in the direction of sociability. Note that within the context of the same sexual instinct the affairs of evolution were also transacted. Sexual mating provided the biological basis to produce new genotypes, childhood the curiosity and carefreeness to explore and experiment with newness, sexual choice the occasion to prefer one phenotype to another. And where new action coordinations (or their physiological or anatomical instruments) were found to contribute to increased reproductive success, a genetic reconstruction assured the safe transmission of the improved genetic package.

Recognizing that with the evolving complexity of the nervous system individual learning became part of the animal's knowledge apparatus, Lorenz yet reached the conclusion that the relative proportions of the hereditary program versus individually acquired information have remained more or less constant: "During all the vast periods of the earth's history, when from proto-organisms well below bacteria our prehuman ancestors evolved, the chain molecules of the genome had the task to conserve knowledge and by suitable investment to enlarge it. And then toward the end of the youngest geological era there suddenly appears an entirely different organic system that sets out to do the same, but do it faster and better" (1973:217).

What Lorenz called here a new biological system of conserving and expanding adaptive knowledge, Piaget (1967) described as the "bursting of instinct." Both biologists saw this innovation as the culmination of an evolutionary trend in which an increase in the regulation of the central nervous system, in the freedom of directed movements and in social cooperation was most conspicuous. Throughout this evolution, Lorenz points out, instinctual drives dominated individual learning.

Specifically in regard to learning, Lorenz elegantly documented how a positive reinforcement that can adaptively modify individual behavior invariably requires an underlying innate drive impulse. In other words, training of a particular response is successful only insofar as the animal can assimilate the new content to the open program of a specific innate action drive. In this connection actions related to the reproductive instinct are singularly immune from imposed modification. Clearly in animals the sexual drive is not open to experimentation. It can be squashed, no doubt, by untoward biological circumstances, as is the unhappy experience of zoos that find their caged animals lacking an adequate drive (or ability) in sexual mating or the rearing of the young. Nevertheless the relatively open program of sociability is precisely in the general area of the sexual instinct. I refer here to the choice of sexual partners and to the regulation of power relations within a social group where individual acquaintance and learning play an indispensable role. Here is the clear beginning of a relating of two individuals, a relating that is oriented in the service of species conservation at the same time as it is the likely occasion of evolutionary expansion. In this manner sexuality is the drive that turns one individual of a species in the direction of another individual, as another of the species; making them sexual partners and cooperative members of a social group, a family of young animals and their caretakers.

My speculation is that humanization continued the trend of sociability, carried up to this point by a genetic program that had already opened up to some individual learning and experiences. However, the opening-up stayed within the confines of actions directly under the control of genetic sexual drives: sexual energy was invested in nothing else than sexual or reproductive-related actions. In humans the energy of the sexual drive—to construct new biological unities and to expand—became separated from its immediate biological aim and available in the investment of a symbolic re-presentation of satisfying social relations. This is the binding of sexual energy, as discussed in chapter 4, which Freud linked with the pleasure principle as the new motivating force underlying symbolic products. The passionate interest in the particular other, so vividly displayed during the courting season of higher animals, is now reenacted on a different level and in biological circumstances that exclude present sexual actions. Everything is there: general bodily excitement, the interest in the other, the intense desire toward the other, "want-my-object"; but that other and that object is reconstructed on a symbolic level as part of a new form of psychological reality.

In the pre-human context, you could say that evolution selected sociability to serve the aim of the sexual drive. With the freeing of sexuality in the human species, the relation of the two is inverted: sexuality is now serving the aim of social cooperation. This, I submit, is the great turning point and justifies the statement that the human brain has evolved in response to an environment of social relations and is specifically adapted to it. This is patently not a fixed reality and even less a particular physical environment, but most definitely a world of ever-changing individual constructions, or better—to indicate that the constructions refer to social relations—a world of social co-constructions.

To this I like to add one of Piaget's favorite statements, which he addressed specifically to Americans always anxious to speed up what he described as a slow development of many years: development is a construction, and biological construction takes its appropriate time. If social relations require personal constructions, then obviously childhood and the successive relation of younger to older generations are indispensable in the formation of sociability. Indeed we cannot fathom what a social world could be that lacked these two ingredients. For that matter a human person is equally unthinkable without a childhood in which the child relates to others of the older and the peer generation.

Some years ago the case of a 13-year-old girl was reported who had grown up in extreme deprivation in terms of human relations (Curtiss 1974). From the age of twenty months she had been kept isolated in a room, curtains closed, herself strapped onto an infant's potty chair by order of her father, who did not want to have any noise or disturbance and who believed her to be dying of some disease. When the father, who clearly suffered from paranoia, died, the mother brought the daughter to the hospital and so the case was discovered. She was found to be severely undernourished, could not stand erect or chew food, had no knowledge of speech, but otherwise was neurologically healthy and according to her drawings and nonverbal tests she was not obviously mentally retarded.

After a brief stay at the hospital, she was transferred to the care of a foster family to help her acquire speech and, above all, social relations of which she lacked even the most primitive rudiments. Her condition is hard to describe. She did not seem to know the functions of other persons, did not, or could not, smile, cry, be angry, or be happy in any communicable manner. She made some remarkable but yet limited progress in coordinated movements and speech comprehension, but quite obviously hers was much more than a language problem. The intense efforts at rehabilitating her were terminated after about three years, and she ended up in the wards of an institution. Lacking the occasions of human relations and its concomitant communication almost from birth, this young woman had no chance to become a person. Without this base her intelligence or language knowledge was of little avail, nor could a training in these turn a nonperson into a person.

How different her fate from other experientially deprived children, such as children deaf or blind from birth! Not only Helen Keller, but many others have become psychologically healthy adults, even though in early childhood they lacked sight or could not avail themselves of a societal language (Furth 1973). Even more remarkable is the case of a 15-month-old infant born with a malformation of the intestines (gastroschisis). With continuous intravenous feeding, Lizzy lacked basic experiences considered in some theories crucial in establishing personal attachment, such as pangs of hunger, pleasure in food, feeling of satiation, the occasional stressful sensations of digestion and elimination. But there she was, a psychologically healthy little person, shy at first, but eventually quite at ease, even when mother left her for a few minutes; sitting on my lap around the lunch table, she played happily with objects I presented to her. As she was enjoying the new activities, she looked proudly around the table as if to say: See how clever I am, see what I can do. Without any knowledge of food or the experience of being fed, she developed well, as do the deaf or blind children mentioned above, in the obligatory context of early interpersonal relations and social and emotional communication. These clinical cases can help make concrete the abstract statement proposed here that personhood, the crucial achievement of humanization, is the psychological co-construction of childhood in an interpersonal and societal context and is primarily dependent on that context almost regardless of particular body and sense experiences.

CHILDHOOD AND HUMANIZATION

From these considerations it is possible to see the connection between childhood and humanization in a new light. Childhood is not a mere contingent period that has to be gone through to get to the really important things that make humans unique, such as conceptual thinking or verbal discourse. On the contrary, these should be regarded as by-products of the developmental process of person formation. Logic, means-end coordinations, communication, sociability—none of these things are unique to humans. The uniqueness begins with the fateful marriage of sexuality and symbol formation when person formation takes on a symbolic character. This is demonstrably true for individual development, and I believe a strong case can be made for evolutionary development. *We became humans, that is, persons, when in childhood we exercised our sexual energies in constructing a symbolic universe,* based on the previous satisfying experiences of bodily interpersonal contact. This, I submit, was the novelty that made the human species unique. For this was the birth of psychology proper, a level of reality not existent for pre-human biology. From that point on, the physical environment was of marginal importance compared to the proper environment of human biology: the symbolic reality in which factual social relations became transformed into personal relations.

You may still wonder why these symbolic transformations should be connected to childhood. It is granted that as a matter of fact they do take place during the early years of children's life. But is there a more convincing necessity? I believe there is, and I mention two relevant points. From a knowledge perspective, symbols in themselves are low-level knowledge products, that is, they do not require more than the logic of the permanent object. Even in relation to what is commonly considered a highly complex symbolic system, namely, societal language, it is known that its acquisition—at least in its more essential grammatical structures—takes place best at ages two to six, long before children are capable of logical reflection. I mentioned earlier that the operations that children begin to master around age seven are precisely the needed instruments to put some logical order into the symbol world.

My reasoning would be as follows. Symbolic material had to be available to provide the occasion in response to which humans constructed the logical systems of concrete and formal operations. But then the first symbols had to be pre-logical, or better, pre-operatory, that is, appropriate to the mentality of a child, not an adult. This argument, I admit, assumes that logical operations are not innately pre-programmed into the brain or simply abstracted from and discovered in ordinary experience. There remains then only one other possibility, namely, that logical operations, like symbols, are products of the active human intellect. This, of course, is Piaget's position as outlined throughout previous discussions and on which more will be said in the last chapters.

The second point, linking childhood and symbol formation, is perhaps intuitively more obvious and compelling. There is, if you reflect on it, something extraordinary, something bordering on craziness, in constructing a symbolic reality. The philosopher Susanne Langer put it well when she considered symbolic rituals as practices

> that are hopelessly inappropriate to the preservation and increase of life. My cat would turn up his nose and tail at them. To regard them as mistaken attempts to control nature, as a result of wrong synapses, or crossed wires in the brain, seems to me to leave the most rational of animals too deep in the slough of error. If a savage in his ignorance of physics tries to make a mountain open its caverns by dancing around it, we must admit with shame that no rat in a psychologist's maze would try such patently ineffectual methods of opening a door. Nor should such experiments be carried on, in the face of failure, for thousands of years; even morons should learn more quickly than that. (1964:41–42)

From the viewpoint of biological actions, which in fact dominated all biology up to the threshold of humans, symbolic reality as such is pure nonsense. If you are hungry, you search for and eat food; if you are angry, you do something in relation to the source of your anger; in either case a symbolic fantasizing or a playful reenactment would serve no purpose, in fact, it would be counterproductive to the biological aim of the respective feelings. And here I repeat a remark made earlier about primate intelligence. It is not so much that primates seem incapable of the object-logic prerequisite to symbol formation, but rather that they exhibit a complete disinterest in using symbols in other than direct physical or social contact.

Compare this to the passionate interest of a four-year-old child in play activity, and you can almost touch the difference between present action reality and symbolic reality. The child desires and gets immense pleasure in symbolically re-living a satisfying experience and assimilates reality to this desire. What is lacking in the primates is this desire. Why is this so? Because the sexual drive—the desire to connect with an other—is not directed toward the construction of a *symbolic* other, but, in good biological tradition, stays within the confines of species-reproductive actions.

It seems evolution could never have succeeded in introducing this biological novelty of symbol making into an adult organism that is preoccupied with the serious business of individual and species survival. The luxury of symbolic play and innocent selfishness had to be started at the childhood stage and consolidated before adult logic and sexuality made their biological claims. Now Freud's constant insistence on the two-phase development of human sexuality can be appreciated in an evolutionary context, and childhood becomes the required preparatory period for constructing the adult person. Another point in Freud's writings becomes clarified. Freud has often been criticized for his singular focus on sexual drives. The standard answer is (somewhat disingenuously) that obviously many other drives are present in humans but they are of no particular interest to the theory. A more relevant reply is suggested by the present discussion of human development and its unique characteristic: the libido-symbol connection in the investment of objects.

I asked earlier how we could envisage humanization, and I was led to suggest that the human childhood phase would have been one conspicuous difference. In the words of Reynolds, quoted above, the best brains of the earliest humans were engaged in sociology. This may be the case, but *all* brains prepared the activity of constructing an adult society when as children they played social relations, that is, acting out symbolically their own childish viewpoints and desires. This playful activity, within the context of present complex social relations and in a state of carefree dependency, ushered in a new sociological and psychological reality. The psychology of individuals in their deepest desires, dreams, values, aspirations, loyalties, and prejudices became then the counterpart of a new sociology, the human society. The instruments of that psychology and sociology were the symbolic products that have their origin in the childhood of each individual. Symbolic rituals and customs held together society and its traditions just as permanent memories and ideals were part of each individual without which they would not be persons.

Marshack (1972) considered the ability to produce and socially share a symbolic story as the chief intellectual and social skill, the primary humanizing tool and technique at the roots of civilization. A story is a prime example of recall memory, a memory that—in contrast to recognition memory—actively binds the past to the present and in anticipation can treat the present as the past of some future time. This time-binding quality is a direct consequence of object and symbol formation; but beside the knowledge component, recall needs the energy of an action-freed sexuality to make the matter recalled a desired object. Almost a century after Freud established that there is no such thing as "free" associations, we are still satisfied to explain our momentary awareness of a past story as something that just happened in our brain rather than as an object we passionately desire, if not today, surely during our childhood.

So the stories Marshack had in mind symbolized objects that were fulfilling the desires of these early children and young people. They listened to and playfully reenacted the lores of fire making, of hunting and gathering, of changing and recurring seasons. And when they grew up, Marshack continued, they were able to recognize significant patterns of physical events or social interactions *in terms of these stories.* With this phrase Marshack touched upon the decisive difference between achievements of sensory evolution (e.g., pattern perception and pattern matching) found at various biological levels, and the human propensity to personalize even the inanimate world. Scholars quoted earlier in the chapter stressed the same point. I would like to remind the readers again that the word "object" used above means a personal object of attachment, or in the language of this essay, a symbolized other in whom sexual energy is invested.

A few comments on art would form a fitting conclusion to the chapter in which the fateful marriage of symbol and sexuality—knowledge and desire separated from present action coordination—is discussed in an evolutionary context. Art is often regarded as a luxury that only a highly developed civilization can afford, a sort of decorative icing on the cake of survival. It somehow does not fit our prejudiced picture of primitive people (savages!), that they should waste their precious time on an apparently useless activity, and we are hesitant to accord them the sensibilities proper to educated persons. Part of the difficulty is our not having a good description, let alone, definition of what art is and how it differs from non-art. But when archeologists discovered exquisite drawings in caves and carved personal adornments or ritual objects dating from 20,000 years ago, some even much, much older, it becomes increasingly unrealistic to link art to a specialized phase of civilization. Rather, art, the pleasure of the human sensibilities in the making and sharing of objects and the impulse to construct such objects must be seen as an integral part of the object forming and symbol forming human psychology.

Marshack (1972) presents fascinating archeological evidence that links art and notation. He believed these artifacts were related to what he had called a "story" and were produced at a time when conceptual notation was not yet clearly articulated (as a mathematical system) just as art was not yet separated from the making of things. Nevertheless, regardless of whether art is a component of a functional production (e.g., the making of an ax), of a symbolic story, of a ritual performance, or simply is nothing else than the joy of making something which is in harmony with our sensibilities, it is perhaps the clearest example yet of the new symbolic-personal reality that attaches to the "object."

As young children begin to become aware of themselves as producers of a world of objects and symbols that is emotionally linked to the first flowering of the eros drive, the experience of the beautiful enters their psychology. This is easily observable in the playful interactions of four-year-old children, who already show strong aesthetic preferences in the making and contemplation of particular sensory configurations. The capability for art is something that requires a protected childhood and a nurturing in its personal-emotional context until cultural education and general knowledge development can expand it into adult social functions. At this early age, there is as yet no clear distinction between personal and impersonal; rather we should consider the entire early symbol world as primarily personal (or social), from which at a later age the impersonal world will separate. In any case, that a biological drive urges the construction and contemplation of a symbolic product and that the pleasure principle can be satisfied in it as an end in itself, indicates the extent of the evolutionary novelty brought about by the freeing of sexuality and of knowledge from present action context and their linkage in the formation of symbols.

6.

Symbols, Biology, and Logical Necessity

THE DISCUSSION SO far has not gone beyond the knowledge capability of six-year old children, and even there the focus was primarily on a form of knowledge that is playful and idiosyncratic, that is, not easily communicable. Here the linkage of personal emotions and knowledge may have appeared entirely convincing. But is not this the obvious reason why philosophers and scholars intent on elucidating knowledge, characteristically typified by science and mathematics, have done well in leaving the childish pre-forms of knowledge aside and staying within the confines of the finished product? The answer is no, to take knowledge out of its historical and developmental context is not only an unjustifiable theoretical abstraction, it is above all a dangerous illusion. Since the earliest days of modern science, it has been shown that rational understanding is immeasurably aided by insights that only a causal-historical inquiry can provide. In addition, we know today that the dividing line between reason and Freudian "rationalization" is far from obvious. Not least due to psychoanalytic insights that have become part of everyday culture, we are prepared to accept that many consciously verbalized opinions are bound to be an inextricable mixture of facts and wishes (whether conscious, preconscious, or unconscious).

But knowledge with a capital "K," objective knowledge on which science is based, surely this is a different thing, with all its safeguards for refutation and verification. With Freud we exclaim: "Our science is not an illusion!" Philosophers of science have probed the nature of scientific knowledge even while science continued its victorious conquest. Through its discoveries we are now in position to destroy not only the entire human species, but along with it the biological-ecological matrix that nurtured the evolution of higher animals and prepared the process of humanization. The freeing of knowledge and sexuality from the context of present action, singled out in chapter 5 as the decisive feature of humanization, has given the new species the awesome freedom over species conservation. This fact is now slowly—too slowly—seeping into human consciousness, and its revolutionary impact is bound to be infinitely greater than any previous world-shaking event.

If you were to ask what it is about scientific knowledge that makes it different from opinions, the popular answer would be that it is impersonal, as impersonal as the facts of nature about which it gives us objective knowledge. The adjective "impersonal" has a wonderfully seductive quality. It gives the illusion of an impersonal objectivity, a reality not merely outside of us, but apart from us, a truth to which we merely submit but have not contributed except in a negative way. In fact, our chief contribution is thought to be precisely to remove our own personal, emotionally linked prejudices and perspectives. The scientific method is accepted as the very instrument to guarantee that we are doing this, or, if by chance we should misuse the method and deceive ourselves, that other people could use it to discover and convince us of our error.

More sophisticated views of science, of whatever persuasion, would stress the naiveté of the opinions expressed in the previous paragraph. In fact, science does not work like this. Two things are generally accepted. A scientific community participates in a particular historical culture, and there is really no way to step out of this personal-social context. Scientific truth is therefore never absolute, it is always relative and potentially changeable. This view of a science that only approaches objectivity recognizes its dependence on social conditions. Another equally popular view in the social-biological sciences links objective knowledge to innate factors localized in the human brain. Individual subjectivity, as well as cultural influences, are believed to be excluded when neurological constellations determine the knowledge product. That genetic mechanisms should have innate knowledge corresponding to the outside world is presented as merely another example of evolutionary adaptation. Objectivity is here linked to evolutionary pre-adaptation.

My aim is not to discuss these views in any detail but merely to examine the models of knowledge they imply. The first view seems to accept social relativity with regret, as if knowledge untouched by humans would be a nice ideal. The second view implies that the encoding of innate knowledge in the brain and the adaptation of a species to its environment comprise an ideal model of objective knowledge and truth. And now compare these models with the "naive" model of knowledge described in the earlier paragraph. You will notice that as models all three views are much the same: all conceive of a prexistent, separate reality. No wonder then that the popular view of objective knowledge as an (ideally) true copy of an outside reality is so pervasive. Everybody ideally seems to want a knowledge that is not influenced by human activity, something as objective as a palpable machine, as factual as the existing species survival.

But for Piaget the objective knowledge of adults is not something coming in from outside that happens to be present to us, but it is primarily a constructive relation of thinking persons, between self and you (singular and plural). Withal it is not a conventional or factual result of things that happen to work in a given situation, but it prescribes to its possessors necessary and universal regulations. Above all it is not just a discovery of an objective reality that is simply there nor is it the free invention of a subjective reality but it is a personal and social co-construction of genuine newness, that is, it is constructive of new reality. Piaget in a unique way opposes to the ideal of impersonal knowledge the proposition that knowledge as such does not exist, but only socially related persons who know.

There is a series of dilemmas, false dilemmas as it will turn out; but nevertheless they are powerful motives that keep the copy model of knowledge alive. One line of reasoning goes like this. If persons construct knowledge, in the first place, this cannot lead to genuine logical necessity, and in the second place, this cannot result in knowledge applicable to nonpersonal things. But these two things happen, *ergo* knowledge is not constructed. Another assumption states that whatever is universal is innate, whatever shows individual differences is learned. But logical reasoning is universal, *ergo* it is innate. These assumptions often are preconscious and work all the more assiduously as they are not fully articulated. Moreover none of the key words such as *knowledge, construction, logic* are unambiguously clear; for that they would have to be anchored in a comprehensive theory. It remains then to delve into Piaget's theory of knowledge and trace the development of logic starting with the child who has attained the object and symbol capability. In doing this I will necessarily touch on the points raised by the above-mentioned assumptions and clarify some of the misunderstandings surrounding Piaget's theory.

THE COORDINATION
OF SYMBOLIC ACTIONS

The symbolic capability provides the two-year-old child with a new psychological reality but not with the instruments to regulate it. Piaget is quite explicit about the new developmental status and the task at hand. Assimilation and accommodation have attained a practical coordination at the final substage of sensorimotor intelligence that places the child firmly into the present world of nearby actions and perception.

Assimilation and accommodation, which have attained a temporary balance at stage VI of sensorimotor intelligence, are again disconnected on the level of representation and language by the intervention of new realities of an extra-perceptive and social order, which again have to be assimilated and explored: to achieve equilibrium on the representative level, a new course has to be run from the start, similar to the one they [assimilation and accommodation] have just achieved. (1946:255)

As the interplay of sensorimotor assimilation and accommodation (outlined in chapter 2) provided a developmental explanation of object and symbol formation, so the interplay of symbolic (or representative) assimilation and accommodation will become the developmental occasion in the construction of mental operations. In contrast to the preceding stage, symbolism requires a double process of accommodations and assimilations. Besides the present accommodation to, say, a piece of wood, previous accommodations (to real airplanes) are conserved in the present so that the piece of wood, moved around in play, also serves as a signifier. The same is true in assimilation; besides the assimilation to the child's present desire to play airplane, previous assimilations (to real airplanes) are conserved in the present so that airplane is "a permanent object" and can become the meaning of the signifier. In this way children playing airplane live both in the present and in the past, or better, symbolically re-live the past.

The same situation becomes even more dramatic when there is no material to play with (no piece of wood), and children play airplane by movements of the arms that imitate movements of the airplane previously perceived. Now previous accommodations are used in the present to serve as signifiers. Finally, diminish the extent of the movements until they are no longer externally observable: children can play airplane in mental imagery still using previous accommodations as signifiers even though they are disconnected from external action. In all three cases, the same double assimilation is at work, a present assimilation ("I want airplane action") linked to previous assimilations (permanent object).

Why do I equate present symbolic assimilation with "I want a specific action," in short, the "want-my-object" of earlier chapters? Strictly speaking, there is no such thing as a symbolic assimilation; the symbolic character of an action is due to its accommodation, which is incomplete, disconnected from the full action, and thereby symbolic or representative.

> A genetic relation can be postulated between operations and the logic of action coordination. For example, the operation of adding two numbers (2 + 3 = 5) derives from the action of uniting things; if one must call this uniting symbolic, this is insofar as the terms 2, 3, 5, +, and = are signs and not things; but the addition that is applied to these signs is as real a uniting in the strict sense as an addition applied to things. (Piaget 1963)

The assimilation of symbolic entities to schemes (and operations constitute indeed particular kinds of schemes) is as real, says Piaget, as is any external action. Hence his constant insistence that thinking is an action, regardless whether it is applied to a present external situation or to an internal symbolized situation. Three-year-old children who play or think of airplane apply the same schemes of airplane to the symbolic material as they would to the perception of a present airplane.

Once the action character of assimilation is grasped, the reason for my putting the "I want" right into the knowledge schemes should become clear. What I am doing is making explicit something Piaget has implicity asserted all along when he referred to knowledge as an action and to the pre-operatory knowledge of small children as egocentric. Egocentric knowledge is centered on the child's own desires, and this means much more than the usual interpretation of "knowledge from the child's own viewpoint." Really, what else should the child do? All *my* knowledge is from *my* viewpoint and all *your* knowledge is from *your* viewpoint. It must be like this if I am not out to deceive you. The crucial issue is, however, what is this viewpoint? On this score the child in constructing symbolic reality is and cannot be anything but ego-centric. Symbolic knowledge is at first "I-want-my-object" knowledge and will remain so for many years to come until the "I" is sufficiently socialized to incorporate the desires and viewpoints of others into itself. When adults use what Piaget calls operations, it is no longer the single "I" who acts but the social "I" (Piaget's "epistemic" subject), who as participant of the group has identified with the knowledge regulations binding on all humans.

Nevertheless symbolism, even the child's most egocentric symbolic thought, is in Piaget's language an elementary expression of the assimilation of affective ("I want") schemes, and as assimilation it is an elementary form of knowledge. It is not non-logical, rather compared to operations it is pre-logical; but in itself it extends the logic of sensorimotor action coordinations and at the least requires, as was said frequently before, the logic of the permanent object. Yet this logic is quite insufficient to coordinate the double processes and differentiations of symbolic reality, and on this score alone there is the impetus to construct the operatory logic adequate to handle symbols. Affective schemes, Piaget says quite clearly, are not something different from knowledge schemes: "All schemes, whatever they are, are at the same time affective and cognitive" (1946:222). Regardless of this plain language, Piaget is not taken at his word. More specially those who compare Freud and Piaget as a rule treat knowledge and emotions as at best comparable, but still as two different things in spite of Piaget's statement that they are different sides of the same coin.

Piaget can partly be blamed for this misunderstanding. First, he is not explicit enough in recognizing the implication of linking personal desire to symbolic thinking, but in addition there are two further reasons. His presentation of logical operations is severely restricted by an abstract and formal language that takes them too much out of the life and blood context of social relations and emotions—even though his final model of equilibration partly remedies this defect. And in his references to Freud's unconscious ("secondary symbolism") he equates it in a cavalier way with the intellective unconscious. "Assimilation is an unconscious process" is a favorite theme in Piaget's writings. Thus, speaking to the American Psychiatric Association (1970), he used examples from what he called the "cognitive unconscious" in trying to persuade his audience that unconsciousness is not limited to the affective domain.

The knowledge schemes Piaget mentioned here are obvious instances of what should be called the preconscious and have nothing to do with the dynamics of the unconscious. Piaget should have known better than to use the slow developmental process of sensorimotor actions becoming conscious as related to Freud's unconscious. By Freud's definition the unconscious does not gradually become conscious; whereas for Piaget children in development draw the conscious ability of logical reason from the preconscious mechanisms of assimilation. Neither will it do to equate repression with the mutual exclusion of knowledge schemes. As Piaget (1976b) himself points out, what people take to be logical impossibility frequently turns out to be a "pseudo-impossibility." Developmental progress is then the transition from impossibility via possibility and probability to logical necessity. Mathematics and science are full of instances of things once considered impossible that later were explored as possibilities and are now recognized as logical necessities. True, when something is considered impossible, we do not spend time and effort thinking of it, but by itself this is not at all similar to Freud's dynamic repression; rather it is a form of preconscious knowledge where the prefix *pre-* has the same developmental meaning as in *prelogical* which Piaget applies to symbolic thought.

Even as Piaget appears quite close to Freud's theory of symbol formation, he merely glosses over the decisive connection between symbol and desire, such as in the following passage where he leaves the crucial choice of a dream unexplained. Speaking of dreams occasioned by bodily impression, he ingenuously compared the dreamer to a baby whose hand is being pinched and, puzzled over the source of the pain, the baby looks around for something to which to accommodate:

> The felt impression searches as it were for a visual correspondence; since the sleeper can see nothing and is unaware of the involvement of the self, yet has the ability to construct images, the person will have recourse to just any image of an external scene provided it has some resemblance. This resemblance implies assimilation of the imagined reality to the internal corporal impression. (1946:215)

Note the phrase "just any image" and resemblance as explanation. This is pure associationism and quite contrary to Piaget's spirit of constructionism. Yet in many other places, Piaget referred to young children's assimilation of symbolic reality to their egocentric desires: "The unconscious symbol is an image whose content is assimilated to the desires of the subject who moreover does not understand its meaning" (p. 219). But, as said before, Piaget never analyzed the psychology of the desire nor did he really understand the dynamics of Freud's unconscious.

For Freud the dream image is invested with unconscious libido, just as are many other things in our psychology that we believe just happen to occur by chance association. He demonstrated that so-called happenings (or mishappenings) in human psychology have a meaning, that is, they are logically connected to preconscious and beyond that to unconscious symbols. These symbols are investments of sexual energy in the construction of a personal world and have their developmental beginnings in the object function and symbol function of the two-year-old child.

While Freud was uniquely interested in this personal, emotional knowledge, he did not hesitate to extend his insights into the psychology of social events as well as products of art or religion. But he stopped short of science. That appeared to him another sort of knowledge, a knowledge cleansed from the obfuscation of the conflicting biological drives ("conflict-free") and solely controlled by logic and objective facts. In short, Freud too worshiped the copy model of objective knowledge and hence could not do otherwise than to contrast emotional from objective knowledge in almost mutually exclusive terms, calling the first illogical, if not antilogical, and reserving logic to the second. I refer to the dilemmas outlined earlier where objective knowledge and personal construction appeared irreconcilable.

Piaget, however, had no qualms about searching for the origins of logic in developmentally earlier forms of knowledge, more specifically, in the logic of biological actions. He demonstrated that there is a functional logic of actions long before the logic of conscious psychology. As a biologist his definition of biological action always included the functional interrelation of the organism and its environment. Action has a functional "meaning," it is teleonomic as biologists would say. The organism "knows" something about the environment and so there is a correspondence (adaptation) between the two. Now there can be no correspondence without a coordination or coregulation. This is where logic and mathematics come in as the formal (i.e., structural) aspect of biological action. There is then a straight line from the logic of genetically programmed action coordinations (instincts) to the logic of genetically open and developmentally acquired sensorimotor action coordinations and finally to the operatory logic of symbolic action coordinations. For Piaget the symbolic actions of children, in their playing and thinking, far from being without logic, are on the contrary the first steps in using logic in symbols; indeed symbols themselves are products of the logic of the permanent object.

Developmental progress from there to the logic of operations does not imply, as it would for those attached to a copy model, a gradual abdication of personal construction, rather the opposite. The children, between ages two to seven, become increasingly aware of their powers of operative construction, and from the logical-mathematical experience, implicitly contained in all symbolic construction, they derive the stuff with which to construct the fully developed operations. The operations then are the endogenous (i.e., deriving from within) interregulations of symbolic knowledge, and through them knowledge can become reflective, fully communicable, scientifically objective, and infinitely open to and constructive of newness.

Before discussing these points at some length later on, reflect that there are two key ways of having assurance that our theoretical knowledge is true and not illusory: logical consistency and social communication. That without achieved operations children cannot have justifiable assurance of logical consistency is self-evident insofar as the operations are the necessary instruments of logical reasoning. This is not to say that a girl, say, age four, before the achievement of concrete operations, cannot reason at all. No, this child has already engaged in symbolic reasoning for some time, and sometimes she is right, sometimes not. But at no time is her reasoning stable, adequately communicable and justifiable, and at all times there is an admixture of irrelevant, if not, illogical elements. Piaget expresses this state of affairs by calling per-operatory reasoning in its first phase prelogical (i.e., partly logical, partly illogical) and later on intuitive (i.e., logical, but still based primarily on perceptive patterns, not on closed logical structures). Social communication is the other necessary condition, not only because of the human proneness to perceptual illusions and to unconscious and preconscious self-deception, but because the operations themselves are interpersonal regulations; they regulate the relations between self and others, insofar as self and others are "human knowers."

But there are yet other and deeper reasons why logic and communication are related and this brings the discussion back to the developmental history of logical thinking. It has its beginning in the "I-want-my-object" desire of small children. Earlier, at the sensorimotor stage, there is logic in action and perception, but there is no thinking. This logic assures the success of the particular action on the particular object of action. But at the symbolic stage, the objects to which children are attached are, above all, other people, or more precisely, the "I" acting in relation to others. The focus is on the other, not on the self; but because the self is only just beginning to be separated from the other, there is a radical confusion between self and other. In their knowledge of the other, the children project their own desires into the object without being aware where self ends and object begins. You can translate this situation in terms of communication and say, the children believe they are communicating with others whereas in large part they are talking to themselves, that is, they are not really communicating. In Piaget's language, they are egocentric and they use logic in an egocentric way.

But if logic and communication are the twin conditions of truth and progress in knowledge, how can the children escape the dilemma they are in, considering that from their viewpoint they are doing both things, namely, being logical and communicative (even though this is more egocentric illusion than reality)? Piaget in his equilibration model (1975) postulates the desire for overall logical coherence, a balance between subject and object (assimilation and accommodation), between and within schemes (differentiation) and a totality balance that in fact is the ultimate coherence motivating knowledge development. But this is not an automatic motivation, as a common misinterpretation of Piaget would imply. Persons become reflectively aware of the knowledge balance only when it is in disequilibrium. A lack or gap in understanding is experienced. This psychological, as a rule preconscious experience of knowledge disturbance is the necessary prerequisite to knowledge development.

A person can respond to the disequilibrium as a developmental occasion and a challenge and consequently restructure the knowledge schemes according to principles intrinsinc to knowledge. In this sense, Piaget asserts, any restructuring is at the same time a functional compensation for a felt knowledge deficiency. But this person can also suppress the negative experience and withdraw psychological energy from the task of restructuring; in this case there is no knowledge development. Piaget always recognized that behind the motivation intrinsic to knowledge development—he called it equilibration—there must be a personal motivation eager to exploit equilibration and expend the required energy.

This personal motivation, however, is social. It is the desire and the knowledge of the "I" relating to and communicating with other people, precisely insofar as the "I" has interest in and respect for the other. In playful symbolism the young children have the I-want-my-object attitude where the I-want prevails over the object. In Piaget's language assimilation prevails over, is not in balance with, accommodation. The children in symbolic play are more interested in their viewpoint than in the object and in this respect there can be no knowledge expansion.

Development in Piaget's equilibration model is predicated on a more radical attitude toward the other, where social solidarity, the interpersonal relation as such is desired. Only then can the knowledge object come into a constructive balance with the socially connected "I." Implicitly the children must want to respect the action and viewpoint of the other and incorporate them into their own viewpoint. This incorporation implies the expenditure of psychological energy for the sake of the I-other relation and constitutes a true co-construction or cooperation. While in itself there is the expansion of an existing interpersonal relation, it is at the same time—and almost as a by-product, at least in early developmental periods—the development of the children's knowledge structures. This in turn enriches their interpersonal relations, a more adequate knowledge leading to better communication and to more fruitful cooperation.

Moreover, knowledge of the other and of self is correlative: children become aware of themselves as persons to the extent that they experience and understand others as persons. With respect to the problem posed earlier why children should be prepared to give up their egocentric viewpoint, Piaget's answer is significant: it is the love and respect of others and the desire to coordinate their own with the other's viewpoint.

Piaget was too good a psychologist to believe that any other reason could motivate young children to experience a knowledge gap and restructure their thinking. In the first place, their logic is yet too weak for them to be bothered (as adults could be) by logical inconsistencies. But in the second place, would not reality itself, the physical environment and its perception, force children to give up a faulty knowledge? The answer is yes, at sensorimotor and biological levels; but on the symbolic plane the impact of the present action reality is severely limited, whereas the human ability for self-deception—or to use a less critical phase, for preferring its own constructed version of social reality—is limitless. Recall the argument of the preceding chapter that social reality is that to which evolution has adapted human psychology. On that base the organic link between symbolization and sociality, and behind that link, the necessary relation of knowledge and interpersonal emotions, becomes comprehensible.

The symbolic world in which all humans live is then the psychological origin of social reality. It includes of course the physical and the biological realities but extends far beyond them. The children's symbolic constructions are the other side of the coin of their social interpersonal constructions. What Piaget is saying is this: without a constructive emotional attitude toward others, children would not construct those symbolic regulations that eventually will become the logical framework of necessary knowledge coordination. He called this framework the system of general mental operations, operations for short, and they are as much the product of knowledge equilibration as of social-emotional interregulation. The phrase knowledge equilibration or coordinations seems to connote an individual affair of internal reasoning and mutual implication within the self. In reality, it is always an active relating of the "I" to other people's viewpoints, it is the coordination, not of some abstract mental entities, but of knowers, that is, people who know and relate to each other.

As you weigh the two contributions, from the social-emotional and from the knowledge side, you begin to have the distinct impression as if the social-emotional component is the more basic in knowledge development. Earlier I referred to knowledge as being almost a by-product of social relations. This is precisely what you would expect if sociability is the principal factor to which humanization was responsive. This evolutionary speculation is also confirmed by Freud's postulating of primal repression and the formation of unconscious symbolism. For these are psychological developments the unique function of which is to produce a deep and lasting emotional attachment to the social group. It is a clear case of knowledge in the service of personal emotions in apparent contrast to the knowledge development described by Piaget. There socialized emotions lead to a logical framework that in itself is free of emotions. (In the abstract: $4 + 7 = 11$, regardless of emotions or social context.)

Similar to Freud's two-phase theory of sexuality, I am then proposing a two-phase construction of symbolic reality. Specifically, I suggest that beginning around age two, children are busy constructing two kinds of social-symbolic worlds, one a world of personal desires and deep social attachments, a private world that as a rule is not intentionally shared with others and that is destined to primal repression; and a different world that, starting like the first, the children are eager to share and that is thereby open to socialization and further knowledge development. As suggested at the end of chapter 3 these two mental realities are constructed concomitantly, but are not clearly separated in the psychology of young children until around age six to seven. At this time they have developed the first fully formed mental operations ("concrete operations") and become aware of themselves as being an "I" who can think and understand. The "I," as the reality ego, stands against that portion of the personal-symbolic world that has not been shared and is now no longer directly open to the socializing influence of others. That portion is now definitely repressed from becoming conscious and communicable. In primal repression the id and its unconscious symbolism are firmly established, in contrast to the ego and its direction to sociability and logical cohesion.

In the id the two basic drives, eros and death, are securely attached to the mental images that symbolize a world satisfying the eros drive, the original motive force for constructing a mental world in the first place. The id remains as the storehouse of libidinal energy, as the model of taking pleasure in constructing a symbolic world and of expanding it in ever new connections, above all, as the prototype of passionate love of the "object." It does not matter that this love in early childhood is as egocentric and the object as unreal (pre-logical) as can be. What matters is a passion for life with other persons, that is, a passion for a personal-social life. If this could be called the aim of humanization, the content of unconscious symbolism satisfies it precisely. With the id solidly grounded, six-year-old children are prepared to abandon their first mental world and conserve it in primary repression. They now transfer the psychological passion of past object-relations into the social direction of that other mental world. This is the "real" world that has been in slow construction all along and in which the children are responsive to intentional communication with others and to logical cohesion.

Having acquired the first instruments of logical control (Piaget's concrete operations), they experience theoretical knowledge as a personal power, which opens for them the exciting world of others. "But now that I am six, I'm as clever as clever" is how they feel, in the words of A. A. Milne (1927); the poet's psychological intuition expresses vividly the children's wish to continue this blissful state "for ever and ever." The passion to expand knowledge and social relations—an emotional-social contribution—is now joined to the children's budding understanding of, and desire for logical consistency. Given these two basic conditions of all knowledge development, the children are in a position to welcome knowledge disequilibrium as an intentional challenge that drives them to compensate for felt knowledge deficiencies. As a consequence, as long as this situation prevails they will develop, as in fact all children do. Development for Piaget can always be regarded in two directions. Looking backward it is a compensation of knowledge structures that are present and felt to be inadequate; looking forward it is a restructuring of these structures and implicates a genuine element of newness, of something that was neither present before nor preprogrammed in physiological structures.

EVOLUTION AND KNOWLEDGE

　　　　This description of knowledge development can be reconciled with an objective logic (and mathematics) binding on all humans—a universal logic—in no other way than to place logic right into species evolution and individual development. This is in fact what Piaget's theory postulates when he equates logic and the coordination of biological action (at whatever stage). Evolution itself as well as individual development can then be conceptualized as productive of new biological realities: new instinct-regulated action coordinations in the form of new species, a new stage of logic in sensorimotor actions, a new psychological reality in object and symbol formation and a new stage of operatory and reflective logic.

　　　　But is not newness limited to evolution, whereas the individual organism is genetically programmed? This would rule out any element of individual choice, even more, any really new actions. There is indeed a vast area of biology where this is true or almost true. Some species have apparently remained unchanged for millions of years. But yet evolutionary changes have taken place and a modicum of genetic reaction norms must everywhere be recognized. In higher animals that are equipped with a central nervous system and capable of free and deliberate movements the fact of a certain genetic open-endedness and individual choice is quite obvious.

In the preceding chapter, the tendency toward open genetic programs was described in connection with the sociability and childhood in the primates nearest to humans. Whether or not their individually developed abilities, their specific choices or inventions, deserve the name of newness, or merely openness relative to the genetic program, need not be decided here. But in the case of humans, the constructing of, first, a symbolic world, then a conscious and logical world, is new not only in the sense of a general evolutionary capability or of an individual developmental re-construction. There is newness also in the stronger sense that these constructions are unthinkable without a previous developmental history (a constructive childhood is necessary) and, above all, that in themselves these are capabilities to generate newness. Thus while knowledge-in-action (biological action) has the tendency to create new forms of life in slow evolutionary history, human knowledge as knowledge-separated-from-action completes this tendency and is by its own working constructive of newness in each individual. And newness, Piaget insists, is the major problem of any theory that claims to be adequate to the psychology of human knowledge.

Evolutionary newness is both a fact and a mystery. Since the time scale and the unit (the genome) is so far from everyday experience, it is no wonder that the ordinary person cannot comprehend its possibility except in the form of grossly simplified and distorted alternatives. It is, properly speaking, a problem of new and of more knowledge. The question is, how did it get into the genome? The two popular alternatives, by God or by chance (chance genetic mutation confirmed by natural selection and survival of the fittest), are evasions and merely testify to our ignorance.

An orchid needs the service of insects to carry the pollen from the male to the female plants. One type of orchid makes use of a contrivance that is shaped like a particular female wasp, and it exudes an odor similar to the female wasp it imitates. In this particular species of wasps, the male wasps hatch before the female. The orchid develops the contrivance at the precise time of the year when the male wasps are alone; without female wasps to attract them, they readily grasp the orchid's contrivance and act as if it were a genuine sexual encounter with the female. However, as soon as the females appear the dummy no longer works and the male wasps are no longer deceived. But in the meantime, the males have been effective intermediaries in the cross-fertilization of these orchids, and the evolutionary function is fulfilled.

This is but one of countless examples where the mind boggles in an attempt to explain how the orchid's genome arrived at the information to imitate a specific female wasp and exercise it at the precise time when the male wasp was around searching for its absent partner. To propose chance mutation as a serious explanation is a pitiful camouflage of ignorance, but it is worse than this. It is a misconception of the nature of knowledge. Knowledge and chance are contradictions. A coin that drops to the ground head up three times in succession has the same chance of landing head up the fourth time as it did the first time, for the coin does not know or remember and this is why it is subject to chance. But is it not possible that a chance event is exploited by the organism and thus leads to new knowledge? Certainly, but now chance is limited to the material occasion, whereas knowledge is shown in the exploitation of the occasion.

If a species knows how to exploit a chance occasion, including a chance mutation, what needs to be explained is the power of exploitation, especially as there are many clear cases where the species actively seems to search for suitable occasions. The polar terms "occasion-exploitation" can be translated in the different language of Piaget as "accommodation-assimilation." A coin is not alive, it does not assimilate or exploit, for it has no knowledge. But the genome is alive and has knowledge and the functioning of knowledge is assimilation. A chance process of knowledge acquisition is a contradiction: it would be an assimilation (since it is knowledge) without assimilation (since it is chance); it makes as little sense as claiming that my knowledge has increased because a book on a topic unfamiliar to me was left by chance in my library.

Starting with his biological perspective of knowledge—as the assimilation of an ecological situation to an organism's action schemes—Piaget (1976a) found it natural to accept modern conceptions of evolution, such as genetic assimilation, the logic of the genes, and the active exploitation of a changed environment. He interpreted these concepts in the same active sense as he did in individual development. For him the comparison of individual and species evolution was more than a figure of speech. Since he insisted that a developing individual constructs anew knowledge capabilities that are considered species specific, he could use the same explanatory principle for the construction of newness by the genome.

One striking phenomenon in which Piaget did some original research is called phenocopy. Genotype is an individual's genetic code, phenotype is the observable end product of that code, considered as due to interaction of the genes and the environment in which the genes function and the individual develops. Phenotypical variations indicate the extent to which the same genetic code is responsive to environmental influences in producing different observable features (anatomical, physiological, behavioral). But only the genotype is inherited and phenotypical variations can have no direct influence on the genotype and consequently on heredity. Taken in a static, absolute sense, this statement leads to the chilling conclusion that the phenotype alone is responsive to the environment but cannot translate this knowledge about the environment to the genotype, which alone is inherited. So we are back at the mystery how the genome (supposed to coordinate the organism's actions on the environment) can do its job unless it obtained knowledge of the environment, and how can this be done if it is supposed not to be responsive to the environment? Against this background the phenocopy is something extraordinary, for here the gene seems to do something it is not supposed to do.

Briefly, Piaget (1974) observed phenotypical variations in the shape of the shell of a particular type of snail as a
function of the calmness or the agitation of the pond in which it
lived. These variations were not hereditary, that is, offspring from
snails with robust shells living in agitated waters, when moved to
calm waters, would have elongated shells and vice versa. This
then is a clear case of phenotypical adaptation; in the language of
knowledge, the snail "knows" something about the environment
and this knowledge is easily explained as due to the individual's
interaction with the environment. It is "exogenous" knowledge,
coming partly from outside, at least with regard to the shape of
the shell (no knowledge is entirely from outside!).

But then Piaget discovered snails that lived in severely
disturbed waters had, as expected, the robust shells. When these
were moved into tranquil waters, lo and behold, the shape of the
shells remained robust and this was passed on to subsequent
generations! So now the variation was no longer phentotypical
but had been stabilized in the genotype. Effectively, the genotype
was imitating a phenotype, hence the name phenocopy.

You may have two snails, both having robust shells,
which in one is a phenotypical, in the other a genotypical feature.
The knowledge of turbulent waters in the phenotype is "exogenous," but in the genotype it is "endogenous". If the origin of the
exogenous knowledge is in the individual's responsiveness to environmental interactions, does it make sense to exclude the genes
from this responsiveness and instead have recourse to a chance
mutation of the genotype that miraculously copies the phenotypical variation?

For Piaget phenocopy is evidence of the genome's responsiveness to environmental influences. He rejected the supposed closedness of the genes as an antibiological, static perspective. Instead he asserted that as the individual in adaptation
assimilates the external environment (movement of the water) to
its scheme of shell formation, so the genome assimilates to itself
(i.e., exploits) the disturbances in its internal environment caused
by the phenotypical messages from the external environment. The
genes' internal environment is the biological context in which

they function, including the physiology of the cells and the history of their development (epigenesis). Admittedly, this is a speculative opinion, but at the least it suggests a possible way in which knowledge from outside can get into the genome (as it obviously does) without having recourse to an extranatural creation or a miraculous chance event.

In this manner Piaget (1976a) regarded the genome as a living system, not a static collection of genetic codes. He speculated that its activity can be likened to a physical combinatorial (Piaget cites the systematic variety of crystal formation) in which the genome explores systematically the possibilities of assimilable environments. Phenocopy would be limited to simple elements of genetic action and would explain the transition from exogenous to endogenous knowledge. The combinatorial would coordinate the elements into genetic programs, whereas the coordination of several programs would result in those complex instinctual action coordinations that interregulate the reciprocal actions of different individuals or even different species, as the orchid-insect relation described earlier.

THE ORIGIN OF LOGICAL NECESSITY

These evolutionary perspectives seem to me crucial for an adequate theory of knowledge even as they extend into biology the speculations of chapter 5 on human evolution. For knowledge and logic did not suddenly appear with humans (or even more restrictively with adult language or science) but they are an integral part of all biology. The most difficult problem must yet be approached head on. Readers should not be surprised that it is *the* problem that exercised the minds of the keenest thinkers for two hundred years up to the time of Kant. Recall that we asked the question how knowledge about the world could get into the organism, how exogenous knowledge could become endogenous knowledge. But all the time we assumed that there was already an organism capable of assimilation and all assimilation implies some form of logical structuring, however implicit it may be. But how did logic get into biology in the first place?

The problem referred to above is the time-honored controversy of empiricism versus rationalism. Historically, it was not couched in biological terms—that perspective came only after Darwin. The issue was the origin of universal and necessary knowledge, roughly the same as what Piaget calls logical-mathematical knowledge and I call logic for short. Note then that the question did not concern specific content knowledge; quite obviously specific content about the known world comes, at least to humans, by way of outside experience, such as knowledge of the color of a mail box, the name of a town, the number sequence of a combination lock. Rather, the question concerned the status of the universal forms of thinking, the rational organization to which all specific knowledge content is putatively assimilated. These forms are experienced by adults as logically necessary and as free of content, binding on all thinking persons, hence universal; they were interpreted as underlying all deductive and inferential reasoning, in particular mathematics and scientific thinking. Piaget called them operations, more specifically logical-mathematical operations, and he studied them in different forms such as the systems of classification, seriation, quantification (concrete operations) as well as combinatorial and propositional reasoning (formal operations).

The philosophers, however, asked no biological or developmental questions, as did Piaget, about these "universals." Instead they speculated philosophically about their reality status and supposed origin. Do they derive from experience or from reason (and ultimately from God who created humans)? If from reason, how is it that they fit experience so well (e.g., mathematics applied in scientific research); if from experience, how can they be universal and necessary (since experience is always of something particular and contingent)? Neither side could resolve their particular problems satisfactorily. Empiricists concluded that there really were no universal and necessary categories—this belief, they asserted, was but a subjective illusion—and so their problem disappeared. Rationalists realized that the introduction of God to harmonize reason and the world was an admission of reason's ignorance to solve their particular problem. The time was ripe for Kant to dismiss both camps as one-sided and suggest a third way to tackle the problem. Kant said yes, there is reason and necessary logic, and this can never have its origin in empirical (i.e., outside) experience; he also affirmed the correspondence between reason and experience. However, this correspondence is due, not as rationalists thought, to divine intervention, but to the *status* of experience: for empirical experience is not, as empiricists would claim, a primary given, rather it is itself overdetermined by rational construction. As Newton turned the universe inside-out and moved the earth around a stationary sun, Kant turned knowledge of the universe inside-out and asserted it is not experience that structures understanding, but it is understanding that structures experience.

Kant's enormous achievements contributed to the demise of the empiricist-rationalist controversy in that he laid bare the inadequacy of either position and pointed to reason's structuring of experience. This direction of rational inquiry was eagerly embraced by Western society and coincided with the explosion of scientific exploration that is continuing to this day. But while Kant on the one hand delivered, as it were, the knowable universe to be subject to human reason—that is what people liked—on the other hand he made reason itself the source of moral, and in some indirect way, of aesthetic norms—and here people could not or would not follow him.

From an historical perspective, Kant had contributed decisively to an understanding of scientific experience; but precisely because of this contribution and the obvious success of science, reason itself became equated with science and separated from the judgment of aesthetic values and the aspiration of moral norms, the very marks of personhood. If today people find it difficult to use the word "knowledge" outside a scientific context, this is a legacy of a trend that itself was responsible for Kant's partial success, at the same time as it reinforced a more basic misunderstanding of his general position. For Kant reason was primarily practical (and this meant related to social-moral actions, not the making of things!), and only secondarily theoretical (instrumental, scientific).

This same trend emptied Kant's subjective structuring of its active meaning and retained only its negative role in the production of "objective" knowledge. Ultimately, the objectivist-realist solution won the day as witnessed by today's popular meaning of subjective as something to avoid in the business of knowledge. The source of objectivity (the only "true" knowledge) is generally accepted to be in the object, where object does not mean (as it does for Kant or Piaget) the object-as-known, but the reality as it exists outside the knower. If there are no universal categories and no necessary logic, then there is no need to search for an explanation of how these things got into human psychology. However, one may be permitted to wonder why all normal adults, scientists and nonscientists alike, should live under the compulsory illusion of logical necessity and use it in everyday reasoning. This perspective is of course the basis for the pervasive "copy model" of knowledge mentioned at the beginning of this chapter.

The cause of the rapid demise of rationalism was the recognition that its postulate of reason was inappropriately tied to the notion of God. With God as creator removed as an acceptable explanation, there seemed to be no source of necessary logic. Anxious to preserve the psychological reality of this logic—in opposition to empiricists who denied this premise—scholars of different persuasion turned to human language in its manifold forms as part of human sociability and culture. The ancient linkage of *logos*, of language and thought, was resurrected. Now logic was thought to be due to linguistic universals, and the search for a universal grammar was on. The acquistion of language was seen as a prerequisite for the acquisition of logical thinking. Speaking of a thing was treated as the crucial event that turned a "percept" into a "concept." Language as an explantory principle of logical objectivity seemed to have additional advantages: it includes the context of a speech community with its implied norms of interpersonal exchanges and above all it can be conserved in oral tradition and in written forms. In the European universities after

Kant, the science of the books (humanistic studies) became separated from the science of nature—another indication that the empiricistic tendency had prevailed and appropriated the name of science in the strict sense.

When in the last quarter of the nineteenth century Freud and, some time later, Piaget turned their research interests toward the psychology of (shall I say?) unconscious and conscious knowledge respectively, they were steeped in the scientific tradition of their times, both having been trained in different branches of biology. Both explored areas that in a sense were taboo. This is clear for Freud. But Piaget too took up an issue that had been buried since the time of Kant, namely the problem of subjects constructing a world of objects. Included in this world would be the knowledge framework of universal categories and necessary logic, which in turn made science possible.

Piaget was profoundly dissatisfied with the prevailing positivistic and humanistic tendencies, whether in science or in philosophy. Without denying the obvious function of societal language, it seemed clear to Piaget, the biologist, that if there is any logic in language itself and in the message it conveys, this logic had been put there by the knowledge abilities of the people who use language and communicate in verbal messages. Going through the *Encyclopedia for Unified Sciences*, the bible of logical positivism, Piaget (1963) was astonished at the insistence with which "logicians, linguists, and psychologist of the school outdo themselves repeating that 'mentalistic' concepts such as thought correspond to nothing, that everything is language, and that the access to logical truth is assured without much ado by a correct use for language." The contrast between the humanists for whom inner experience and inner language is everything and the positivists for whom mentalistic concepts correspond to nothing is striking, but the convergent manner in which both misuse the concept of language is all the more blatant.

If there were any shred of truth in the necessary connection between societal language and logical thinking, the extensive research with profoundly deaf children who lack knowledge of a societal language should have indicated some systematic

logical deficiencies. On the contrary, these children showed remarkable comparability with the developmental acquisitions of
hearing children (Furth 1966, 1971). Such massive results would
be more than enough to convince anyone seriously interested in
logical thinking that its source had to be searched for in other
areas than societal language. But the copy model of "objective"
knowledge and truth is so appealing and the admixture of the
active subject in their construction so repugnant to what parades
as common sense that facts alone will never change a person's
knowledge theory.

> If truth is not a copy, it is then an organization of the real. But an
> organization on the part of what kind of a subject? . . . Philosophers
> . . . place truth beyond spatio-temporal and physical contingencies
> and make "nature" intelligible in a timeless or eternal perspective.
> . . . Unfortunately, from Plato to Husserl, the transcendent subject
> has constantly changed its appearance, without any other progress
> except that due to the sciences themselves, hence to the real model
> and not the transcendent model. . . . It may be worthwhile, before
> placing the absolute in the clouds, to look into the interior of things.
> Moreover, if truth is an organization of the real, the preliminary
> question concerns the understanding of how an organization is
> organized. This is a biological question. . . . But if it is characteristic
> of life constantly to evolve further and if one looks for the secret of
> the rational organization in the biological organization *including its
> evolving,* the method then consists in trying to understand knowl-
> edge by its own construction. This is reasonable since knowledge
> is essentially a construction. (1967a:413)

Kant knew that knowledge—scientific knowledge—
is a construction, the structuring of empirical experience according
to what he called *a priori* categories. What he did not know or
concern himself with was the origin of these categories. With
Darwin behind him, Piaget knew that *a priori* can only refer to a
structural knowledge prerequisite, not to a temporal sequence and
that the knowledge structure itself must have a biological history.
Furthermore, he viewed logical necessity as correlative to the
potential freedom to construct novelty; this explains why as a

biologist almost single-handedly he insisted on the reality of logical necessity and rejected any watering down or relativizing of
the categorical logic. This is the taboo to which I referred earlier.

We are today uncomfortable with any categorical absolutes; they remind us too much of totalitarian doctrines and
blind imposition of faith. The evils done in the name of absolutes
are only too apparent to the student of history. But there is a basic
misunderstanding in this analogy. The *a priori* categories of logical
necessity by themselves are no knowledge, they are procedures
empowering you to understand something and go beyond the
given to construct newness; but in themselves they are empty.
Their use and application is a personal, free, and therefore moral
decision. Moreover, the operations are not imposed as something
you suffer from outside; and in this respect your brain and your
physiology is as much outside of yourself as is the external content
of knowledge. The logic of the neuron is still a long way from
being my logic nor is the chemistry knowledge of my intestines
my knowledge of chemistry.

Consistently with this position Piaget rejected a theory
of evolution that proposed chance mutation and survival of the
fittest as the only source of new knowledge and instead outlined
a view, as summarized earlier, that accorded to the genome a
more active role. He likewise criticized the hypothetical realism of
K. Lorenz, who treated human logical operations on the same
level as any other evolutionary product and referred to them as
working hypotheses confirmed by successful adaptation. Not
chance and external necessity, but freedom and internal necessity
are for Piaget the twin biological conditions of new knowledge.
Biological freedom means primarily openness from innately programmed action coordinations. Moreover, the greater the freedom
the more complete must be the regulations that coordinate the
organism. Corresponding to the radical freedom of human knowledge to explore and construct limitless new realities is the perfection of its regulations, namely, the operations. They form a closed
but at the same time mobile system of logically necessary implications that gives us the possibility and experience of our freedom;
in fact, this is our freedom, as it is the base of our autonomous

knowledge for which we can be responsible and provide justification.

　　Piaget's task of elucidating the Kantian program—and it should be clear that Piaget's work is a deliberate continuation of the philosopher's insights—is not yet over with the demonstration of the developmental history of logically necessary operations. If the source of logic cannot legitimately be attributed to the outside intervention of a divine creator (idealism, rationalism), the experience of objects (empiricism), inner experience (humanism), the language of society (logical positivism), the genetic program (innatism), the adaptation of evolution (hypothetical realism), where is it found? From the last quote Piaget's answer refers to "the biological organization including its evolving," that is, in the language used earlier, "constructive assimilation." As said repeatedly, assimilation means the action of the organism on the environment: the organism does something to the environment which as a consequence participates in the organism's organization. There is an element of logical structuring in all assimilation, and there is a potential openness for expansion that is most conspicuous in evolutionary and developmental construction.

　　Piaget's argument seems to be this. Logical necessity cannot derive from any content or object, for it belongs to the abstract reality of organization, not to the concrete reality of organized things. A biological organization interacts with the environment for its biological purpose. This interaction implies content knowledge about the environment and organizational knowledge about incorporating environmental elements into its own organization. The first kind of knowledge focuses on the outward-directed process of accommodation to the environment, the second on the inward-directed process of assimilation to the internal organization. Being alive, both processes are potentially open for expansion as new forms of accommodations provide the need and the occasion for new forms of assimilation. While the material for new *accommodations* derives from outside, that is, the environmental objects and resistances, the material for new *assimilations* derives from inside, that is, from the biological organization itself.

　　New assimilation means a new organization, and this comes about through an internal restructuring. At all times knowledge is a structuring (relative to the biological organization), at privileged times when the conditions are ripe and in response to felt resistances, knowledge becomes a restructuring and this means a restructuring of the organization. This then is evolution or development: it is not something that happens to knowledge from outside, but it is the life of knowledge itself. The conscious regulations of operations (i.e., the psychological experience of logical necessity) derive therefore from the laws of biological organizations and their constructive assimilations. Moreover, since logical necessity as a psychological experience belongs to the symbolic realm, individual development of a symbolic world, and the occasions and challenges of this world are a prerequisite.

In summary, and in contrast to most others, Piaget in his constructivist theory of knowledge acknowledges the existence and the need of universal categories of necessary logic (operations) through which the limitless openness and fecundity of human knowledge is assured. The operations themselves cannot but be individually constructed; this is done by children in their development beyond object and symbol formation. The ultimate source of logic is the biological process of assimilation, which at all times is constructive according to the organism's organization and on challenging occasions leads to a restructuring of that organization. In themselves the operations are the completion of laws and tendencies present in developmentally more primitive biological regulations. All assimilations (i.e., organism-environment exchanges) presuppose instruments of assimilation (i.e., schemes) that in turn must be integrated in the organism's overall organization. This requires regulations. But regulations always imply some logical coordinations, between organism and context, input and output, means and ends. Therefore logic is always within the organism, not as an abstract category, conceptualized by human thinking, but as a living regulation within evolution and development, and it is primarily enriched through its own life, not through imposition of any outside contribution. This is how Piaget, the biologist, can see a way of reconciling the apparent paradox philosophers could state but not resolve: the status of logical necessity in relation to empirical reality.

Indeed, Piaget's lifelong aspiration was to pave the

way toward a science of knowledge that would include a whole
gamut of empirical disciplines, notably biology, psychology, sociology, cybernetics, history of science. It would acknowledge the
legitimate problems philosophers of the past and present had
raised, but it would apply empirical methods to their solution. The
method of choice would be to study the historical formation of
knowledge in the interdisciplinary context of the aforementioned
sciences. As he said, the fruitfulness of this approach hinges on
the claim that "knowledge itself is a construction."

The use of the term *construction* implies not only logic
but also the expenditure of energy. Not by chance did Piaget
consider the construction of newness the proper function of
knowledge, and his theory is specifically framed to make the
synthesis of logic and newness comprehensible. Thus knowledge
as the necessary framework for organism-context interactions
draws its enriching material from its own functioning. It is autonomous in the sense of being self-regulatory. But at the same time
the energy to expand, to conquer increasingly more environmental interactions, is within knowledge from its biological beginning.
The libido-symbol link that I described earlier as characteristic of
human knowledge is itself the evolutionary expansion of a connection between knowledge and motivation which for biological
thinking is a matter of course.

Knowledge as a coordination of a biological action
requires by itself no more motivation than biology itself. Philosophers correctly understood that with human object-formation
the organic link between knowledge and action had been broken.
But they failed to realize that this separation made the connection
between knowledge and eros, the drive to expand, all the more
tighter. The scope of expansion is now infinitely wider and the
environmental object has become interwoven with the ever-
changing interpersonal relations between self and others. To take
human knowledge out of its human context is an illusion precisely
because knowledge *is* (the construction of) this human-social
context.

All scientists and scholars who ever had an original
thought, all artists who communicated their creative vision, all

social and moral leaders who constructively responded to challenging circumstances, material or social, indeed all humans who relate in novel forms to others, are passionately involved with their objects. They could not have done so if they did not live in a symbolic world of their own making to which they are emotionally attached in a most intensive way. Combined with this necessary emotional connection to the deepest personal drives (safely repressed in each person's unconscious psychology), there is the possibility of a measure of social control and of conscious, personal responsibility. This possibility is the direct consequence of the necessary logic that belongs to the psychology of the developed person.

Piaget's operations are the rock bottom smallest common denominator of the "I-to-you" relation. On the basis of their inherent logical necessity, I can hope to establish a free personal relation with you, whoever you are. And insofar as personal interactions are constructive of the relation, there is co-construction and cooperation, and this is precisely what operations are. To put this adequately into practice is an ideal that, like truth, we can approach but never reach. But there is hardly a greater obstacle to this constant endeavor than the truncated notion of a knowledge that does not constantly have to be nourished by positive emotional interrelations. Construction of knowledge and construction of personal interrelations are two sides of the same coin.

In the Piagetian perspective of this chapter the logic of assimilation is proposed as coinciding with the origins of biology. In chapter 5 I marshaled arguments for the view that social cooperation stands at the threshold of humanization. From these two premises it follows that for humans the principles of both logic and morality are indeed autonomous. This means, from a developmental viewpoint, that their acquisition in childhood cannot be in the form of learning some contingent content or information; rather they must derive from within the sphere in which they function, namely, existing personal relations and interactions. This will be the theme of the final chapter.

The logic of operations and the principles of cooperation are reciprocally related. Normative moral values result from an evolutionary tendency to develop in the direction of obligatory social relations, the reciprocal side of the tendency to develop in the direction of necessary logic. The difference between the normative values of logic and of morality would reflect their respective sources: logic binding absolutely, even evolution itself, morality binding relative to the biological function of human evolution. With the ultimate collapse of human cooperation the disappearance of persons and morality is conceivable but, for what it is worth, logical necessity would survive in the context of the remaining biological assimilation.

7.

Logic and Desire

PIAGET'S THEORY IS widely criticized, even by writers sympathetic to his constructivist perspective, for neglecting social and emotional components. In a superficial sense this criticism is justified. Clearly Piaget's primary aim was to focus on the categories of necessary logic and to explore their derivation from biology (psychogenesis), and these categories—in themselves—are universal, that is, they are the same regardless of social or emotional contexts. Writers who are willing to concede some form of intrinsic relativity (if only the version appealing to biologists and philosophical pragmatists: logic is valid because it works) seem much more sensitive to social and emotional dimensions. But this is not a solution to the problem, this is the removal of the problem. Certainly, Piaget's theory stands or falls with the genuineness of the problem of universal categories. If they do not exist, if they are but psychological illusions fostered by biological, social, or economic conditions, not only the theory but autonomous reason itself is superfluous.

It is also true that Piaget has not written extensively, nor explored experimentally—with one notable exception—in the social-emotional domain. The one exception is his work on the child's development of moral understanding, written (like almost everything else in this area) when he was still in his thirties, well before his discovery of the logical properties of concrete operations and his love affair with logical groups and systems. When interviewed about this early work some forty years later (Evans 1973:37) he smilingly shrugged it off as something not to be taken too seriously, as a diversion in response to a colleague of his who challenged him whether his theory could be applied to the field of values. On different occasions during his later life, Piaget (1952) referred to his entire early work that used the clinical interview technique in almost apologetic terms. Nevertheless, these were the books that established his early fame as a child psychologist. Yet Piaget's ambition as we know was far more in the direction of philosophical and biological issues, and the public did not take kindly to what appeared to be a change away from psychology. For almost thirty years, his work was largely neglected and its rediscovery in the United States coincided with the post-Sputnik area of educational reform. The paradoxical result: whereas Piaget addressed his work to philosophers and scholars in natural sciences and the history of science, it was school teachers clamoring for a better theory of education who assured his present popularity.

It is easy to interpret the older Piaget's attitude about his early work as an indirect form of resentment for present and past misunderstandings ("you liked my first studies, but neglected my later work; yet this first work is really not very good"); but there are probably more deep-seated reasons for Piaget's not continuing his explorations of knowledge in relation to the social-emotional areas. Like any genuine innovator, Piaget must have realized that the inclusion of these questions could lead to an ever-widening scope (as Freud found when he discovered unconscious forces in all of psychology) and would not permit him to focus on the key problem on the nature and formation of logical operations.

It is almost trivial to add that there were also personal reasons in his case (as there are in Freud's or anyone else's case). Piaget (1952) spoke openly about his flight into intellectual activity and writing as an early defense against an emotionally unstable mother who combined neurotic tendencies and religious earnestness (the typical patient Freud encountered). As a young man, he went through a period of restless activity in different fields and indicated by his writings a remarkable degree of social and ethical ideals—remember also that he had some personal experience of psychoanalysis—but when he had finally found what his life work would be, he increasingly avoided becoming preoccupied with social-emotional issues. So we are left with a series of isolated statements, like unfinished works of art; by themselves, I would agree, they hardly suffice to make his theory relevant to emotions and sociability.

LOGIC: THE MORALITY
OF SYMBOLIC THOUGHT

Nevertheless, as I attempted to show, a deeper understanding of his theory makes it clear that Piaget's epistemic subject is indeed the socially connected, emotionally committed, and morally autonomous person as described in previous chapters. So I would say, Piaget did not finish his work, of course not; there remains plenty to do to establish genetic epistemology as a legitimate science in the manner Piaget had hoped. But I could hardly find a more urgent task than that of integrating the psychoanalytic insights into unconscious psychology and the theory of (conscious) logical knowledge. This morally beautiful person who is the epistemic subject (or the subject of any other ideal-type theory) is still a person of flesh and blood who would not be socially connected or emotionally committed without the basis of an unconscious psychology. Moreover, this unconscious world is individually developed and is a far cry from an ideal rationality, far from logical consistency or moral integrity, it is, as Freud said, a whirlpool of personal conflicts and selfish desires. And yet—it is the indispensable basis for becoming a person. We should be rightly suspicious, as was Freud, of any theory that depicts rational persons without recognizing explicitly the conflicting unconscious drives in their psychology.

Even though Piaget misunderstood Freud's dynamic unconscious (as explained earlier) the theory of object permanence and symbol formation clearly points to the first developmental connection between knowledge, emotions, and sociability: "The ability to conserve feelings makes interpersonal and moral feelings possible" (Piaget 1954:44–45). Here are the three areas juxtaposed: "to conserve" means to reconstruct symbolically, i.e., *to know*, and *emotions* are at the base of *interpersonal* relations. And where do these emotions originate? "From feelings of good will toward persons who have given pleasure." Piaget described the object of this pleasure: it is "not the enrichment that each partner draws from the other but the reciprocity of values and attitudes," implicit in interpersonal exchange.

There is a crucial difference between instrumental or means-end relations, as developed in typical sensorimotor actions, and interpersonal relations that are built on the reciprocal formation of symbolized values and attitudes. These symbols are a source of pleasure and the first objects of drive investment. After several years of accumulating and intercoordinating these positive interpersonal feelings within the protective context of family dependency, children around age six are prepared to enter the reality of the wider world, the world of things and the world of persons (peers, society). Both in the physical and the social world the children are beginning to recognize norms that derive from the relations themselves. Piaget connects organically these two worlds by one of those statements mentioned earlier that surround his theory like signposts to a promised land, but are not elaborated: "Morality is a logic of action in the same way that logic is a morality of thought" (1954:13). This statement, like the earlier ones, comes from Piaget's 1953 lectures on intelligence and affectivity. It is, however, first found some twenty years earlier in his book on the moral judgment of the child.

There Piaget (1932) studied children's judgments of right or wrong and confirmed what others had suspected before him, that there are two kinds of morality, one based on relations of conformity and unilateral respect, the other on relations of reciprocity and mutual respect. Because of the condition of childhood, social life necessarily begins in unilateral respect which throughout life in one form or another will always express the pressure of the older on the younger generation. But side by side there is another form of social life where partners are co-equals and where the norms of their relations are worked out in mutual cooperation. This is what Piaget observed in the games of young children. On this evidence he argued forcefully for the spontaneous development of the morality of cooperation in contrast to the imposed morality of conformity. He rejected the notion that the latter gradually merges with the former as if the morality of cooperation could be imposed from outside; rather he held that both forms are present in all concrete instances of social life. However, the cooperative form alone, Piaget held, assures that personal and societal relations can develop toward a morality of cooperation as the ideal form of equilibrium.

Piaget therefore discovered in social relations the same developmental law of expanding autoregulation (or equilibration) that he ascribed to knowledge development. Clearly too the two different norms of sociability could be called exogenous (from outside) and endogenous (from inside) respectively, and thereby the connection between social development and evolutionary development (discussed in chapter 6) also becomes apparent. Note however, that "inside" does not mean within the individual, but within the interpersonal relations, that is, within the "reciprocity of values and attitudes" mentioned above. In the 1932 work, Piaget implied that social cooperation in terms of intellectual exchange could perhaps explain the logical structures: in other words, reflection on social cooperation would lead to logical operations. Twenty years later he had changed his view and criticized what he did earlier:

I satisfied my need for an explanation in terms of structures-of-the-whole by studying the social aspect of thought (which is a necessary aspect, I still believe, of the formation of logical operations). The ideal equilibrium pertains here to the cooperation between individuals who become autonomous by this very cooperation. (1952)

In the meantime Piaget had discovered the roots of logic, long before the possibility of intellectual verbal exchange, in the concrete operations of seven-year-old children and even before the acquisition of language in the sensorimotor actions of infants. New also was his theory of object- and symbol-formation. Eventually, as we know, he would postulate the presence of logic in the biological organization itself. He now considered conscious logical operations and social cooperations as two co-equal achievements of equilibration so that neither one can explain the other.

With respect to social cooperation itself, Piaget—for personal and strategic reasons mentioned earlier—never went beyond this global statement, and he did not spell out further implications. Yet there were two additional contributions that Piaget recognized as potentially relevant, namely symbol formation (1946) and his theory on the reciprocal formation of social values (1965). As shown above, he linked interpersonal and moral feelings with the developing object and symbol formation, and this is where reciprocal social value and "good will toward persons who have given pleasure" is first formed. Here then is the germ of both morality and conscious logic.

But whereas Piaget patiently traced the steps from the logic of sensorimotor actions to explicit logical operations, nothing comparable was done regarding morality. This essay can be considered an attempt to fill this gap. Hence my concern to relate Piaget's explanation of the symbolic function to the richness of the symbolic-emotional world as described by Freud. Beyond that I wanted to show that sociability, the pleasure of interpersonal relations, is indeed an end in itself and I suggested that anthropological studies on humanization also point in this direction.

When morality is called the logic of action, the meaning of "action" is interpersonal relations or actions within the social context of other people's actions. But when logic is called the morality of thought, the content to which logic is directed is the instrumental relation of human actions on things or the complementary reactions of things. In instrumental actions we seek success; reflecting on action coordinations we can reach conscious logical operations, and they in turn can be applied to the understanding of new instrumental actions. In interpersonal actions, however, we seek primarily the sharing of symbolic values, which is the foundation of personal relations. This is accomplished, as shown in chapters 2 through 4, by the construction of a symbolic world; it is the main task of early childhood and probably the main task of humanization (chapter 5).

In the course of development and in adult societal life, interpersonal and instrumental actions are increasingly intertwined, and cooperation in the double sense of reciprocal mutual relations and a logically consistent working together on a given problem is indeed a desirable ideal. But there remains the difference between reflection on instrumental and on interpersonal actions; reflection on interpersonal relations is much more complex, much less imposed by external necessity and, above all, in itself more alien to the action that it reflects. To take the last point first, and abstracting from the artistic-aesthetic component inherent in actions: understanding the mechanics of an instrumental action and doing the action successfully both share in the same "objectifying" attitude toward the action, namely success and control; understanding a personal-social relation or a moral situation is, however, something quite different from being in the relation or in the situation—as Freud would say, to know something by hearing of it or by experiencing it are two quite different psychological phenomena.

This connects with the other points concerning interpersonal knowledge. Here Freud again has shown that the sources of personal and social interrelations are to a great extent unconscious (not merely, as in the case of instrumental relations, preconscious); reflections in these psychological regions are necessarily limited and personally most laborious. Finally, survival and sheer material necessity frequently impose reflections to anticipate error and assure success of instrumental actions. In social and personal relations, on the contrary, there are almost always strong traditional forces of compulsion and conformity, or what I would like to call "the social unconscious." This works directly against the attitude of mutual equality and reciprocity required for constructive reflection.

In what sense then is logic a morality of thought? Recall that Piaget's theory is principally concerned with knowledge insofar as it is constructive and productive of newness.

Knowledge that has become thoroughly habitual and routine is indeed a poor shadowy trace of its real capacity and requires in itself no other explanation than adequate attention to the problem and a well-exercised network of neural pathways. But knowledge in its formation is another matter; there the capacity can be studied in its full strength. That is why the observation of knowledge acquisition—whether in the individual or in society—is not merely fruitful but cannot be replaced by any other method.

But surely, you would interject, a six-year-old girl who comes to understand the operations of numbers, is not discovering something new; just as learning today the earth moves round the sun is not the same as the new insight of Copernicus. Yes and no. A first discovery is different and we call it an original creation of a genius. It requires a rare combination of personal and societal conditions along with overcoming the weight of habitual thinking. However, one thing is clear. The new object of knowledge would have never been grasped unless its creators had a passionate personal relation to it that provided the drive and the commitment to risk the unknown and turn possibility into a new reality.

The girl learning numbers is of course in a different position. Above all, society rewards her for acquiring what by now has become habitual societal knowledge. Yet from her own perspective there is personal newness; she has to give up her own cherished beliefs—which in themselves were past personal achievements that had become habitual—and reconstruct a new knowledge organization in response to something proposed to her by society of which she wants to be a part. In her too there is passion and commitment, albeit not to an unusual degree, and hence we are apt not to notice it. All children use their knowledge in its full strength (this has nothing to do with "optimal potential"), including passion and commitment, and for this and no other reason they develop.

As children get older and turn into adolescents and young people, their individual psychological organization of knowledge, personal relations, and emotions becomes more and more tightly interrelated and, thanks largely to the achievement of logical operations, stabilized. With advancing age what I have

called knowledge-in-its-full-strength becomes increasingly difficult and therefore rarer. Consequently, at an adult level newness
in knowledge is not something easily or quickly achieved. As a
life event, this newness usually takes months and years to come
to fruition, and societal constraints and opportunities play an
indispensable role.

I have used the words "passion" and "commitment"
in connection with knowledge development. I should be more
explicit and call these things by their real names. "Commitment"
is precisely the morality of symbolic thought as the attitude required to participate in the community of thinking persons and
abide by the norms intrinsic to knowledge. Knowledge, as Piaget
always implied, is an interpersonal relation; it is a co-construction
and a cooperation and implies at all times the coordination of
different viewpoints. But the general principles of conscious logic
or morality are in themselves action-disconnected. Passion is required to connect you as a particular person to the particular
objects of your action. The object has to be "real" to you. In this
connection logical and social objectivity are largely irrelevant, as
is the entire psychology of what Freud called secondary processes.
What counts here is the pleasure reality of the infantile world
which is indelibly conserved in your unconscious id.

Socialized and sublimated in part (as the ego), the id
is the ultimate ground which determines whether you assimilate
defensively and restrictively according to the logic of things or
constructively according to the logic of life. "To act according to
the logic of life against the logic of things is the whole of morality,"
wrote Piaget, the young biologist, in the aftermath of the senseless
slaughter of World War I. And for the next sixty years his single-
minded aim was to construct a theory of knowledge that was
based on assimilation, the logic of biological action.

In his favorite role as the most severe critic of "Piaget's
theory," he published in 1975 an entirely new version of his
equilibration model. In it he referred to the equilibration of cognitive structures as the central problem of development. (Note the
implied equation of knowledge with development.) This model,
briefly sketched above, brings to life the logic of assimilating in-

dividuals who are driven to explore new observables and open up new possibilities—a far cry from Piaget's former mechanistic model of probabilities and logical dimensions.

In the same vein, shortly before his death, he recognized the shortcomings of his earlier formalized description of logical operations. They were "too closely linked to the traditional models of extensional logic and truth tables [i.e., the logic of things]. A better way, I now believe, of capturing the natural growth of logical thinking in the child is to pursue a kind of logic of meanings . . . meaning is never isolated, but always inserted into a system of meanings, with reciprocal implications" (Piaget 1980:5).

A logic of symbolic meaning is precisely what the present synthesis of Freud and Piaget postulates. Within each individual "the system of meanings with reciprocal implications" reaches back to its developmental beginnings at which time the child, driven by the desire of "want-my-object," first discovered the meaning of symbols in the pleasure of the object-found-again.

KNOWLEDGE AS LOGIC VERSUS
KNOWLEDGE AS DESIRE

Piaget's basic assumptions concerning knowledge as the general coordination of present or possible actions have been discussed throughout this essay. From this assumption it seems a small step to identify knowledge with logical structure: every coordination has a logical structure. In this view is knowledge then effectively nothing but logic and logical compositions? To this straightforward question Piaget would have to say "yes," or rather "yes, but . . . ," for he would insist on two or three crucial preconditions. First, *knowledge* intended in this question signifies at most the empty procedure of a possible knowledge; second, the concept of *logic* is not to be limited to formal propositional logic, rather it must be extended to any system within which logical

composition obtains, as for instance, the coordination of sensorimotor actions. In addition there is a third condition, namely, that
the phrase "of an action" is implicity added to the above equation
of knowledge and logic. If these conditions are made explicit, the
pale abstraction of equating knowledge with logic gives way to
the rich concreteness of real or possible actions.

In this world of action, Piaget recognized a first division
of logical structures: those that coordinate biologically pre-programmed actions and those that are open to individual development. He referred to this as the "bursting" of the instinct. On the
far side of this division, there is evolutionarily acquired innate
knowledge, on the other side there is developmentally acquired
action knowledge. A second division of logical structures is relevant to human development and it occupied a major portion of
this essay, namely the division into sensorimotor and operatory
structures. The former coordinate present actions, the latter (operations including preoperations) coordinate possible actions. In
the language of this essay, the first is action knowledge proper,
the second is object knowledge. The first division implied the
bursting of an innate knowledge program, the second division too
entails a psychological break which was explained as the separation of the object of action from the present action, thus consti-
tuting the separate object of knowledge.

Symbol formation becomes then possible insofar as
the symbolic product is the concrete reconstruction of an object
of knowledge. Clearly, without the logical capability of object
knowledge, there can be no symbol. In turn, the development
from object knowledge in its first symbolic manifestation to the
fully achieved structures of logical operations—subjectively experienced as logical necessity—covers an age span of ten to fifteen
years.

In this precis of Piaget's developmental theory, knowledge, notwithstanding the inclusion of its action direction, remains
abstract and not adequately connected to the individual. Readers
of Piaget who criticize his theory as overly intellectual and as
socially and emotionally sterile usually limit their view to this
logical side; in addition they fail to appreciate the constructive

action character of this logic. Piaget's theory is not, and was never meant to be, an adequate psychology of human knowledge in all its myriad forms. By design he explored with single-minded purpose the nature and the developmental genesis of the general logical structures that made that psychology possible. In the hands of Piaget, the perspective of equating logical structure and knowledge yielded a research program of vast scope with a host of subsequent empirical and theoretical insights comparable to only one other program in modern psychology, namely the work of Freud.

This should suffice to demonstrate the fruitfulness of Piaget's initial design. But there is a price to be paid for single-minded direction, and both Freud and Piaget had to pay the cost. One result is that neither are comfortably included in the academic science of psychology. A more serious drawback is a one-sided reception of Piaget's work which turns his logical assumptions into trivial clichès or incomprehensible caricatures. In the way Piaget's theory is frequently presented, the negative comments made against it seem to me to be entirely justified. Why is there this vast discrepancy in interpretation and, from my viewpoint, why are the very points of the theory that seem fruitful and exciting so difficult to share and make comprehensible?

Logic in the sense of a formalized system is readily accepted. The computer revolution has made possible complex logical model building at the same time as it facilitated the exploration of the central nervous system in a manner unthinkable a short time ago. These two branches of scientific endeavor—information processing and brain research—are in tune with modern computer technology and the information revolution which is changing our public and personal life. The logic of computer programming and information processing is indeed the logic of things and it conforms to a formalized system. There is no place for the libido of concrete action, for the desires and emotions that breathe life into the logical framework.

While both Piaget and modern cognitive science seem to focus on logic in their basic assumptions, they treat logic in diametrically opposed ways. For Piaget logic, specifically the explicit logic of the adult scientist, is something that has to be explained. What is logic in relation to knowledge in general? How does it function, and what are the chief products of logic? These questions are quite alien to cognitive science as it is engaged in the construction of logical models. Piaget's assumption that knowledge be equated with the logic of action resulted not only in a vast expansion of research relevant to psychology and biology, but also severely limited the subject matter of the investigation. This is not an accidental coincidence. Scientific progress always has been accompanied by a delimitation of the object of exploration.

In contrast, the object of cognitive science is as vague and as ill defined as the noun from which it borrowed its name. *Cognition* is simply another word for knowledge; it has the added convenience of lending itself to the linguistic formation of an adjective and a verb and—an old trick of psychology—of being a technical term. It promises to avoid entanglement with the connotations of everyday language. Another technical term is of course *information* and what can be done with it in the brain or the computer: storage, retrieval, processing. For cognitive science, logic in the form of formalized logic is a tool in terms of logical-mathematical models, and its object is as vast and undefinable as the innumerable objects of knowledge. For Piaget, however, logic, as the general coordination of all biological action, is the precise object of his research, and he employed a biological model of adaptation and of evolutionary or individual development. Whereas information scientists start with information, the object of knowledge, as something given, Piaget starts with the biological capability of logic through which the organism constructs the information, the object of knowledge, in the first place. To assimilate an object is to structure an object, and there can be no structuring without logical composition.

Kant said he had to limit science in order to make room for faith. So, it seems to me, Piaget limited knowledge to logical structuring and thereby made room for the relative freedom and the driving emotions that are present in all human knowledge. From a knowledge viewpoint, an object for Piaget is something that is assimilated, and that means it is structured according to the logical structures of the schemes; but from the object viewpoint it is at the same time something that is selected and desired to which the subject wants to accommodate available knowledge schemes. The strategy of limiting knowledge to the logical component has indeed paid off handsomely in permitting us to understand the merger of knowledge and desire in the concrete knowledge object. This merger is patently obvious in the symbolic world that two-year-old children begin to construct. And at this age it need hardly be emphasized that the objects of knowledge are objects of intense desire or that they are also radically personal, or better, interpersonal objects. "Want-my-object" is the child's primary knowledge attitude, in which it is not easy to demarcate separate components of logic, of desire, of interpersonal relations.

Scholars reflecting on human knowledge *per se* have never felt comfortable with this picture of a child's knowledge. They would readily agree that at a young age children's knowledge is inextricably mixed up with personal desires. For this reason they are unsympathetic to the use of the word *knowledge* for children or animals and would prefer to limit it to the objective knowledge recognized in the adult world. Similarly, they dislike the concept of a general symbolic function that includes gestures, imagination, dreams, and societal language. The reason for these concerns is obvious: language and objective knowledge according to them belong in a separate category quite distinct from the symbolic-personal-emotional products typical of childhood. For them and for most people in our culture, Popper's division of reality into three worlds is quite comprehensible and unobjectionable: the world of physical reality, the world of subjective personal products, the world of objective personal products. This last world, called "World 3," would comprise science, art, and other lasting cultural achievements.

As a biologist Piaget would have difficulties with the first division. Where do living beings below persons fit into the scheme? Moreover, does it make sense to separate the organism from the biological context in which it lives? But the focus of the present discussion is the distinction of World 3 and its implied immunity from personal subjective desire (which would corrupt its so-called objectivity). Why this pervasive fear of subjectivity and this misreading of subjective actions? Is Beethoven's music any the less beautiful, is Newton's gravitational theory any the less objective, because the authors may have been driven by unconscious incestuous or paricidal desires?

Piaget's theory of the development of logical knowledge structures is a theory of organic continuities. So is Freud's theory of primal repression of the child's symbolic world and the subsequent sublimation of drives. Stage progression for Piaget never meant the total elimination of lower levels—we could not function as humans without sensorimotor actions or pre-operatory symbols and values—but their (always partial) incorporation in a restructuring at a higher level. Repression for Freud never meant the final elimination of childish drives and desires; if anything it stressed its opposite, their permanent conservation in a person's unconscious psychology. In both theories intense desires and emotions toward other people are the context and condition of development. This personal attachment and its developmental history constitutes what is commonly called a child's socialization.

Object knowledge and symbol formation provide the logical structures through which children can re-enact and re-present their attachments, "want-my-object," as their subjective psychological reality (is this the start of Popper's World 2?). The children gradually come to recognize the self as the agent of the acts and desires, just as they come to recognize others as persons with their own acts and desires. In addition there are other objects that are regularly perceived as unable to act or desire on their own but yet are mysteriously related (e.g., belong to, can only be used for) to persons. The desire to deepen and extend this attachment is the dynamic psychological force, indispensable for increased knowledge and symbol formation in general as well as for a more differentiated knowledge of other persons and self. Interpersonal communication and the sharing of actions, critically present from birth, take on a new character as children come to use language in a fully symbolic manner. The knowledge object is then not only separated from present means-end actions but also from present means-end needs, that is, interpersonal relations are an end in itself.

Between ages five and seven the socialization of children reaches a critical developmental threshold. They are at the point of experiencing the impact of their first logical operations, that is, the autonomous operations of logical necessity and inference. They are poised at entering the real social world and are emotionally ready to let go of their private, egocentric world constructed over the past years. In Piaget's language they are achieving the first concrete operations, in Freud's language they experience the collapse of their oedipal world (primal repressions) and are on the path toward drive sublimation (along with the constitution of the superego). Now these two attitudes—toward logical consistency and toward the viewpoint of other persons—are precisely the two sole criteria that can lead to rational objectivity.

World 3 objectivity is therefore not something outside human passion and desire; it started in each child's development with the intense pleasure in logical consistency and in the sharing with (and approval of) others and the correlative displeasure of experiencing logical inconsistency and inability to share. These attitudes remain at the source of all cultural, artistic, and knowledge achievements. And primal repression, that is, the definite formation of the unconscious id, is at the same time the definite opening of the ego toward a full knowledge rationality and a socialized reality, which are both based on autonomy and mutual reciprocity.

Sublimated in the context of drives means socialized, just as *real* in the context of knowledge and reality means socialized. It seems almost perverse even to suggest that the socialized person should be free of attachment to others, albeit this is asserted only in connection with the person intent on improving and searching for knowledge. Nothing was further from Piaget's mind than the caricature of a formal thinker, caring for nothing but his or her own formal context-free logical structures and constructing some new insight on the strength of personal introspection. What, in fact, is an object of formal thinking? Unfortunately the word "formal" suggests a decontextualized something, abstracted above all from emotional and social biases and expressed in precise, symbolic propositions. The tendency is to forget that these propositions on which formal thinking operates are always the subjective constructions of a thinking person, even more so, if one could say so, than in concrete operations which imply a present or possible accommodation to concrete events. Indeed, in formal thinking the direct object to which we accommodate are other (real or hypothetical) people whose thinking we respect. *Respect* is used here in the sense of taking seriously, not in the sense of approving.

If the adult logical operations are in fact a certain final achievement of logical closure and completeness—at the same time as they are the obligatory instruments of logical necessity and unlimited openness—the fundamental "function" of knowledge can be seen to coincide with the evolutionary function of humanization, sketched in chapter 5. On the object side of accommodation, knowledge is inextricably linked to cooperation with and respect for (the viewpoint of) other persons. On the subject side of assimilation, there are structures of context-free and necessary logical composition which may give the illusion of an autonomy not dependent on the judgment of others. That this is an illusion cannot be logically demonstrated (as Kant was at pains to point out). But history in the inclusive sense of the history of ideas and ideologies attests both to the power of the illusion and to its fallible results. This in itself would not be so bad; after all, we can learn from our mistakes. But the fallible results have not been limited to knowledge; bad knowledge and bad actions have frequently gone together. The organic connection between knowledge and action, so frequently denied in theoretical speculations, is constantly evident in the concrete history of societies and of individuals. "What biology has put together let no speculation put asunder."

But is not this precisely what Piaget seems to have done? And what stronger evidence for it can be produced than the statement at the beginning of this section, his guiding assumption of equating knowledge and logical structure? Here, I believe, we put our finger on the crux of misunderstandings that saddle many interpretations of Piaget's theory and almost turn it into its opposite. As I attempted to make clear earlier, limiting knowledge to its general logical structure is decidedly not the same as constructing a logical model of knowledge. Piaget unswervingly used a biological model and accordingly conceptualized knowledge as a reciprocal organism-context relation between knower and known (between agent and object of action, between subject and object of knowledge).

By studying knowledge under the precise aspect of logic, he could accomplish two almost contradictory things. He could extend logical structures right into biological actions, long before there could be any meaningful attribution of articulated logical consciousness. At the same time, he could endorse an adult logical understanding that derives its overriding necessity from its own principles and in this sense is context-free. Consistent with this view, he found himself in the unpopular position of having to oppose the neo-Darwinian chorus of those who treat logic as an evolutionary result. His claim was, as shown in chapter 6, that a necessary context-free logic can never have its source in the contingent evolution of this context. For similar reasons he rejected the equally popular opinion that children's acquisition and use of societal language could adequately explain the emergence of adult logical thinking.

Earlier in this section, we agreed that Piaget's equation of knowledge with logical structures, even with the addition of that which is being structured, namely, logical structures of present or possible action, was still too general and one-sided and liable to be misunderstood. Its connection with the concrete social person was not expressed. Undeniably, Piaget's own manner of constantly focusing on logical assimilation combined with a comparative neglect of accommodation has contributed to the frequent misunderstandings. Nevertheless, Piaget's presentation of knowledge as logic makes it possible to refer meaningfully to knowledge as desire without either having to empty logic of its necessary procedural rationality or desire of its unconscious libido toward a concrete object. By conceptually isolating the logical direction of assimilation from irrelevant contingencies, whether of the individual or of culture, and by insisting on the autonomous mode of its evolution and development, we can use the very closure and context-free necessity of the logical system as the stable anchor against which personal freedom and desire can come into play.

Accommodation is in fact the missing link in the presentation and understanding of Piaget's theory. It is the reciprocal direction to assimilation. Every object of assimilation is also, and at the same time, an object of accommodation. Behind every assimilation there is the closure of logical coordination and logical composition, and here Piaget felt at home. Behind every accommodation, however, there is the indefinite openness, indeed the potential chaos, of individual desire and choice. While Piaget referred to knowledge schemes as instruments of assimilation, he was careful to point out that it would not make sense to call them instruments of accommodations. Yet he did not hesitate to say that every knowledge scheme is also an affective scheme. What, in fact, would correspond to instruments of openness to others? Here we must leave the domain of knowledge and have recourse to Freud's language of drives and desires.

The same drives that motivated children in the first place to disconnect sensorimotor action and knowledge and to become emotionally attached to the personal symbolic constructions must eventually be transferred to a wider social reality. This is Freud's clear message of sublimation, which the public has always been happy to consider in its negative aspect—the reality control of the unruly id—but is loath to accept in its positive dynamics. Desire and knowledge were linked when around age two libido was bound through symbols. A sublimated drive is still a desire and adult knowledge-in-its-full-strength, though it may be action-disconnected, or rather precisely because of this, must be emotionally connected to the unconscious id. Creative artists are known to have this knowledge-id connection to an unusual degree. The symbolic world within which they create is as intensely real to them as is the first symbolic world to all children.

Freud has shown that the morality of the superego is connected to the unconscious forces of the id; a morality that pretends to be alien from unconscious emotions is not only dishonest, it is in the long run both individually and socially destructive. My aim in this essay was to propose that in the radical constructivism of Piaget's theory we have perhaps for the first time a perspective that not only admits but indeed postulates the necessary connection between biological drives and the logic of conscious knowledge. As with Freud's morality, when knowledge tries to hide its libidinous origin, it is cut off from its constructive energy and is left to operate in a restrictive and ultimately destructive manner. Far from being opposed to each other, human emotions and knowledge, desire and object, are two sides of the same coin and have their common origin in the biological evolution of human sociability and in the individual development of each child. The acceptance of this view could, I believe, contribute toward an honest appraisal of the function and limit of personal and societal knowledge. This would seem a necessary prerequisite to the responsible social use of this knowledge and its implicit power. Piaget's is perhaps a timely theory for a knowledge that has reached its present constructive and destructive power.

References

Bringuier, J. C. 1980. *Conversations with Jean Piaget*. Chicago: University of Chicago Press.

Curtiss, S., V. Fromkin, S. Krashen, D. Rigler, and M. Rigler. 1974. The linguistic development of Genie. *Language*, vol. 50, no. 3.

Evans, R. I. 1973. *Jean Piaget: The Man and His Ideas*. New York: Dutton.

Fisher H. 1982. *The Sex Contract: The Evolution of Human Behavior*. New York: Morrow.

Freud, S. 1895. Project for a scientific psychology. In *Standard Edition of the Complete Psychological Works of Sigmund Freud*. 24 vols. James Strachey, tr. and ed. London: Hogarth Press, 1953–1974.

—— *Gesammelte Werke*. 18 vols. Anna Freud et al., eds. London: Imago, 1940–1951.

1900. The interpretation of dreams.

1912. A note on the unconscious in psychoanalysis.

1913. An evidential dream.

1914. On narcissism: An introduction.

1915a. Instincts and their vissitudes.

1915b. Repression.

1915c. The unconscious.

1918. From the history of an infantile neurosis.

1920. Beyond the pleasure principle.

1924a. The dissolution of the Oedipus complex.

1924b. A short account of psychoanalysis.

1925. Negation.

1926. Inhibitions, symptoms and anxiety.

1927. The future of an illusion.

1933. New introductory lectures.

Furth, H. G. 1966. *Thinking Without Language: Psychological Implications of Deafness.* New York: Free Press.

—— 1973. *Deafness and Learning: A Psychosocial Approach.* Belmont, Calif.: Wadsworth.

—— 1981. *Piaget and Knowledge: Theoretical Foundations.* 2d ed. Chicago: University of Chicago Press.

—— 1983. Symbol formation: Where Freud and Piaget meet. *Human Development*, vol. 26, no. 1.

—— 1983. Freud, Piaget, and Macmurray: A theory of knowledge from the standpoint of personal relations. *New Ideas in Psychology*, vol. 1, no. 1.

Humphrey, N. K. 1976. The social function of intellect. In P. P. G. Bateson and R. A. Hinde. *Growing Points in Ethology.* Cambridge: Cambridge University Press.

Kant, I. 1786. Putative beginnings of the history of humankind. In *Werke.* 6 vols. W. Weischedel, ed. Wiesbaden, Germany: Insel, 1960.

LaBarre, W. 1954. *The Human Animal.* Chicago: University of Chicago Press.

Langer, S. K. 1964. *Philosophy in a New Key: A Study in the Symbolism of Reason, Rite and Art.* New York: New American Library.

Lorenz, K. 1973. *The Dark Side of the Mirror: Essay in the Natural History of Human Intelligence.* New York: Harcourt Brace Jovanovich, 1977.

Mahler, M., F. Pine, and A. Bergman. 1975. *The Psychological Birth of the Human Infant: Symbiosis and Individuation.* New York: Basic Books.

Marshack, A. 1972. *The Roots of Civilization.* New York: McGraw Hill.

Milne, A. A. 1927. *Now We Are Six.* New York: Dutton.

Piaget, J. 1932. *The Moral Judgment of the Child.* New York: Free Press, 1965.

—— 1936. *The Origins of Intelligence in Children.* New York: Norton, 1963.

—— 1937. *The Construction of Reality in the Child.* New York: Basic Books, 1954.

—— 1946. *Play, Dreams and Imitation in Childhood.* New York: Norton, 1951

—— 1952. *Autobiography.* (Reprinted in Evans, 1973)

—— 1954. *Intelligence and Affectivity: Their Relationship During Child Development.* Palo Alto, Calif.: Annual Reviews Monographs, 1981.

—— 1963. Language and Intellectual Operations. (Translated in Furth, 1981).

—— 1965. *Études sociologiques.* Geneva: Droz.

—— 1967. *Biology and Knowledge: An Essay on the Relations Between Organic Regulations and Cognitive Processes.* Chicago: University of Chicago Press, 1971.

—— 1970. Affective unconscious and cognitive unconscious. In *The Child and Reality: Problems of Genetic Psychology.* New York: Grossman, 1973.

—— 1974. *Adaptation and Intelligence: Organic Selection and Phenocopy.* Chicago: University of Chicago Press, 1980.

—— 1975. *The Equilibration of Cognitive Structures: The Central Problem of Development.* Chicago: University of Chicago Press, 1985.

—— 1976a. *Behavior and Evolution.* New York: Pantheon Books, 1978.

—— 1976b. The possible, the impossible, and the necessary. In F. B. Murray, ed, *The Impact of Piagetian Theory*. Baltimore: University Park Press, 1979.

—— 1980. Recent studies in genetic epistemology. *Cahiers de la fondation des archives Jean Piaget*, no. 1.

Reynolds, V. 1976. *The Biology of Human Actions*. San Francisco: Freeman.

NOTE. In published translations the original's exact meanings and fine distinctions, critical for a theory of knowledge, easily get blurred. For this reason the translations in this essay from the following texts are my own: all of Freud except Freud 1895, Kant 1786, Lorenz 1973, Piaget 1946, 1963, 1967, 1975.

Index